Judd

I really APPRECIATE You reading
my book. THANK You

All the Best

PRAISE FOR MILLION DOLLAR BRONZE STAR

"A side of the Vietnam war not yet told and an amazing example of courage during an unpopular time in our Nation's history."

— Jody and Bryan Rodriguez

"A young man's insight to do the right thing, not only led to a bronze star but a successful future"

— Heather and John Fahey

"A hero in our eyes always and your memoir portrays just that. A man willing to fight for your country, and do it with honor, courage and grace."

— Sara and Chris Boyd

PRAISE FOR MILLION DOLLAR BRONZE STAR

"The title had me at 'debauchery,' but the amazing story throughout paints a vivid, personal picture of a tour in Vietnam and the life of high character and accomplishment it formed."

— Clarke Michalak, CFA
PGIM Real Estate

"Bruce's story is one of courage and inspiration to serve with excellence and face fear regardless of the possible outcomes."

— Mark Vande Hey
Executive Director, PGIM Real Estate

"An engaging story of an American soldier in Vietnam battling the consequences of doing the harder right over the easy wrong in a corrupt setting... with his life on the line."

— Steve Ernst
*Executive Director of Transaction Management
for Global Occupier Services, Cushman & Wakefield*

"Engaging story of a soldier serving his country in unusual circumstances during an unpopular war. A real story from a true hero and patriot."

— John B. Jackson, SIOR, CCIM
Director of Industrial & Land Services, Cushman & Wakefield

"A captivating story of Vietnam many may not know about and sadly I'm sure much of this continues today."

— Dale Taysom
Real Estate Professional with PGIM (aka Prudential)

MILLION DOLLAR BRONZE STAR

A SOLDIER'S STORY OF CORRUPTION AND DEBAUCHERY IN VIETNAM

BY
F. BRUCE LAUER

TACTICAL 16 PUBLISHING

MILLION DOLLAR BRONZE STAR:

A Soldier's Story of Corruption and Debauchery in Vietnam
A Memoir by F. Bruce Lauer

First Edition

Because of the dynamic nature of the internet, any web address or links contained in this book may have changed since publication and may no longer be valid.

The views expressed in this work are solely those of the author and do not necessarily reflect the views of the publisher, and the publisher hereby disclaims any responsibility for them.

Published by Tactical 16, LLC
Monument, CO

ISBN: 978-1-943226-43-6 (paperback)

This book is dedicated to my loving wife, Barbara, and our four amazing children: Heather and her husband, John; Jody and her husband, Bryan; Sarah and her husband, Chris; and our son, Bryan, who passed away at the age of thirty-six.

In addition, this book is dedicated to our nine grandchildren, who light up our lives: Lane, Avery, Paige, Braden, Payton, Carson, Jack, Clara, and Chase.

A Special Tribute to my Mother,
Mary Lou Thompson

It is with pure joy that I thank my mom from the bottom of my heart for what she has provided to me and my family. My mother has always been there for us through thick and thin. As she approaches her 92nd birthday, we look forward to celebrating that one with many more to come.

We love you, Mom.

A Special Thanks

I would like to thank Tyler Killette, who assisted me greatly in getting this book to the finish line..

CONTENTS

INTRODUCTION

This book, *"Million Dollar Bronze Star: A Soldier's Story of Corruption and Debauchery in Vietnam,"* is F. Bruce Lauer's account of the eleven months and nineteen days he spent in the Republic of South Vietnam as a soldier in the Americal Division. He shares stories about his life leading up to Vietnam — from his sheltered childhood in  Mansfield, Ohio to the stricter-than-bootcamp halls of Bob Jones University, to landing what he thought was his dream job in accounting before a draft letter brought everything to a halt. Bruce also shares his experiences during the rigors of basic training, advanced training, and war — and ultimately his return to civilian life and a successful career in commercial real estate.

During his service in the U.S. Army, Bruce learned about survival, loss, and sacrifice in an environment of lawlessness, corruption, and debauchery that was foreign to him in a number of ways. Often funny and always sincere, Bruce's book reflects on his personal experience as a soldier and how that ultimately shaped who he would become as a husband, father, friend, and business leader.

A NOTE FROM THE AUTHOR: DISCLAIMER

I borrowed this disclaimer from another military memoir by Major General Lloyd B. Ramsey: "Many of these events are described from memory and may not be correct, especially places, dates, and, in some cases, names. Most of the notes on military events, places, and dates are from histories and should be correct. However, some of my descriptions of the events are based on my memory and should be judged accordingly."

"I have not received permission to use anything that I have copied from histories, other books, magazines, newspapers..." except the book, *Brokers Who Dominate*, which I have Rod Santomassimo's permission to use. "When I have quoted from a document, I have given the document credit. I have also published a list of acknowledgements."

PREFACE

This book came into being primarily because of the gentle nudging of one of my daughters, Jody. On a rather persistent basis over the years, as I would share my war stories, she would say, "Dad, your stories about what you saw during your stint in the Army are fascinating to us and would be to everyone — you should write them down."

Thus, the seeds were planted, and I began the process of writing a story that portrays my three years and one week in Uncle Sam's Army. Never once while in the Army during the Vietnam War did it occur to me that I would someday put the pen to paper to drill down and tell my story. But fifty years later, it's time to move forward.

From the sands of Fort Jackson, South Carolina to the Quartermaster School in Fort Lee, Virginia, onward to Tan Son Nhut Air Force Base in Saigon, to the white sands of Chu Lai, and back to Fort Benning, Georgia, my experience in the Army was not your typical story of a young G.I. And given the life expectancy of an 11 Bravo, which you will learn later in this book, I am grateful for that. I was not on the so-called front lines, and I have but a few harrowing tales of combat to share. But this, I assure you, does not mean my time in the Army was humdrum or without turmoil. And it certainly does not mean I wasn't afraid for my life every hour of every day.

However, instead of accounts of close calls with the enemy, this book focuses more on what goes on behind the scenes of an American war zone, or in my case specifically, of the club system for the Americal Division in Chu Lai, Vietnam. Looking back, my exploits and encounters in the Army were probably especially interesting to my daughter Jody and others who know me well because danger and debauchery are so unlike my character and so opposite my life both before and after I served. Up to the beginning of Basic Combat Training, I had led a very sheltered life. Things changed for me very quickly. Marked by graft, greed and corruption, my experiences during those three-plus years in Uncle Sam's Army would affect me forever, in ways I never imagined.

Serving in the Army was both a duty and privilege. It was a formative part of my life and an eye-opening venture into the "real world" that had a profound effect on who I became as a husband, father, friend, and businessman. These accounts will be shocking to some and painfully familiar to others. In either case, I hope you will read with an enquiring mind and an appreciation for all those who have bravely served this great country.

MILLION DOLLAR BRONZE STAR

A SOLDIER'S STORY OF CORRUPTION AND DEBAUCHERY IN VIETNAM

BY
F. BRUCE LAUER

CHAPTER 1

HIGH SCHOOL

I graduated from Malabar High School in Mansfield, Ohio in 1964. I was one of approximately 208 students who made up the school's first graduating class, as the school had only opened its doors in September of 1963.

At this time, the conflict in Vietnam had been going on for nearly ten years. The draft was in place by the time I graduated, and all through my high school years, I knew there was a possibility I would receive a letter from Uncle Sam the day I turned eighteen. Some of my fellow classmates found themselves in this situation. A few found ways to avoid being drafted, from fleeing to Canada to botching their physicals. But many others served and, sadly, several never made it home.

Fortunately, I had always planned to go to college and get good grades, and I knew that as long as I followed that plan, I had at least four years until I would find myself in Vietnam. At that time, draft-eligible men could receive a deferment while attending college as long they kept their grades up. Let me be clear: I did not have any reluctance toward serving in the military. If I had been drafted on my eighteenth birthday, I would have proudly served my country then. However, it was also important to me that I would be able to support my family, and to do that I would need a college degree. I was a good student, ranking in the top 10 percent of my high school class, and I had no reason to believe I wouldn't do just as well at the university level.

I was ultimately drafted the year after graduating college, just before the lottery system was put in place. By that time, I'd spent four years at a small, religious university that, in many ways, was more militant than the military.

WARE'S FANCY FRUIT

From the age of sixteen I held a number of odd jobs that showed me the value of a college education. During my junior year at Malabar High School, I worked at a place called Ware's Fancy Fruits, a specialty grocery store that catered to the eccentric buyer of oddball food items. I was connected with the store's owners, Irma and Earl Ware, through a woman named Winogene Wade, who was the mother of my high school sweetheart and future wife, Barbara. My initial pay was sixty cents an hour, and after I'd been there for six months, I got a nickel per hour raise. While I found this job to be mostly banal, it did come with a great perk. As someone with a fair knowledge of coins, I made a deal with the owners regarding coins the store received as payment. Should any coin come into the grocery store that I wanted for my collection, I simply had to pay them the face value for it. One Saturday morning, I hit the jackpot when an elderly lady paid her bill with five Liberty Standing Quarters that were in mint condition. These coins, featuring the Goddess of Liberty on one side and an eagle in flight on the other, were only struck between 1916 and 1930. These coins were so valuable that they equaled more than the six months of pay I'd earned on the job so far. I stayed at Ware's for another two months to enjoy my extra nickel an hour for hitting the six-month mark, then decided to rack up my work experience as a down payment toward my future. This also opened up my free time to play high school baseball.

WORKING WITH THOMAS ALAN GETZ (TAG)

One of my close high school friends, Thomas Alan Getz, or TAG for short, offered me a job with him cleaning a two-story office building for $100 per month. This building had several tenants, which included the IRS. After we had completed the first month, Tom's dad paid him the $100 and Tom then paid me $45. I looked at my friend and said to him, "You shorted me $5."

Thomas Getz

My friend's reply was that since he had found the account, he deserved a bigger piece. So, he got to keep his $55 and I got $45. That was my first time experiencing that not everyone has the same idea of what's fair, and it taught me to always have everything in writing when it came to business situations. Tom was always a stand-up guy, and I don't think he was intentionally trying to cheat me. This was just an early example of his skills as a businessman in an area that I clearly had much to learn.

Later, Tom and I would end up serving in Vietnam at the same time. We were stationed in different areas, but occasionally wrote letters to keep in touch with one another. Tom was a conscientious objector, which means he was an individual who claimed the right to refuse to bear arms while serving in the military on the grounds of personal freedom of thought or conscience. In order to perform his duty with the U.S. Army, he served as a medic. In his letters, Tom would talk about his days in the battlefield patching up soldiers, both U.S. and Vietnamese. Regardless of which side they were fighting on, Tom would help whoever needed it. That was just his nature.

CLASSMATES WHO WENT TO WAR

Tom was not the only friend of mine to end up serving in Vietnam.

Of the soldiers who went to South Vietnam from Mansfield, Ohio, thirty-four did not return alive. Of them, two were my high school classmates: Joseph Denig and David Winder.

JOSEPH DENIG

Joseph Henry Denig and I were very close during our high school days. On frequent occasions, we would play baseball in an open field along with his younger brother, and Joseph's dad would join us on a regular basis. I remember Joe always had a smile on his face. He also had a genuine desire to help anyone and he was always supportive and encouraging to everyone he was around.[1]

Joseph Denig[3]

I was stationed in Fort Benning, Georgia after my return from Chu Lai, South Vietnam in March of 1970 when I heard the news of Joe's demise. My mom sent me a rather lengthy article from the *Mansfield News Journal* that told of

Joe's dying while serving his country. From what I understand, Joe had just boarded a helicopter and as it reached 150 feet, it was hit by enemy fire and crashed. The three crewmen were wounded in this incident, and First Lieutenant Joseph Henry Denig was killed.[2] Even though it's been more than forty-nine years since Joe's demise, I still think of him often, particularly when we play sandlot baseball or softball. Joe was a true high school friend and his engaging smile will never be forgotten.

PERSONAL DATA

Home of Record:	Mansfield, OH
Date of Birth:	Monday, 08/05/1946

MILITARY DATA

Service:	Army (Reserve)
Grade at Loss:	O2
Rank:	First Lieutenant
ID No:	292442941
MOS:	1542 Infantry Unit Commander
Length of Service:	*Not recorded*
Unit:	Mobile Advisory Team 88, MACV Advisors

CASUALTY DATA

Start Tour:	Friday, 05/08/1970
Casualty Date:	Thursday, 08/20/1970
Age at Loss:	24
Remains:	Body Recovered
Location:	Gia Dinh, South Vietnam
Type:	Hostile, died
Reason:	Air loss, crash – land – helicopter-non-crew

ON THE WALL: Panel 08W Line 125

4

DAVID F. WINDER

David Winder[4]

David was another high school classmate of mine, and we both graduated in June of 1964. During our high school days, I recall David always being around the athletes. David was a skinny little redhead, and although he was not selected to play on a team, he was part of the team by serving as team manager. I lost contact with David after high school, but years later, I learned of his exploits and ultimate death in an unusual way.

I am somewhat of a Vietnam nut and over the years have read many, many stories covering the gamut of activities in the Republic of South Vietnam. I was in a bookstore several years ago and in the war section saw the book *Vietnam Medal of Honor Heroes* by Edward F. Murphy. It had excerpts about approximately half of the 200 or so individuals who were awarded the Congressional Medal of Honor while doing their duty in Southeast Asia. While reading it, I came to the story of a Medal of Honor recipient named David Winder. When I first saw his name at the top of this excerpt, I said to myself, "No way this could be the same Winder that I knew from Mansfield, Ohio." But as I read on, I realized that this David Winder was in fact one and the same. If, in high school, you would have told me that David Winder was going to be awarded the Congressional Medal of Honor, I probably would not have believed you.

David's Medal of Honor citation, which goes into some detail of how he earned this honor, certainly pulled at the strings of my heart as I read about what he so courageously did during the firefight that ultimately took his life. I am forever awed and thankful for what he did for me and for our country. David Winder is a true hero and I'm proud to say that I knew him.

PERSONAL DATA:
Home of Record: Mansfield, OH
Date of Birth: Saturday, 08/10/1946

MILITARY DATA:

Service:	Army of the United States
Grade at Loss:	E3
Rank:	Private First Class
ID No:	292444402
MOS:	91A10 Medical Corpsman
Length of Service:	*Not recorded*
Unit:	HHC, 3rd Bn, 1st Infantry, 11th Infantry Bde, American Div, USARV

CASUALTY DATA:

Start Tour:	Saturday, 11/22/1969
Incident Date:	Wednesday, 05/13/1970
Casualty Date:	Wednesday, 05/13/1970
Age at Loss:	23
Location:	Quang Ngai Province, South Vietnam
Remains:	Body Recovered
Casualty Type:	Hostile, died outright
Casualty Reason:	Ground casualty
Casualty Detail:	Gun or small arms fire

ON THE WALL: Panel W10 Line 37

DAVID BEARD

David Beard

David Beard was the president of our high school class. He was a good friend of mine and an excellent athlete. After we graduated high school in 1964, David went to the Naval Academy, and later became a jet fighter pilot for the Marine Corps. We served in Vietnam at the same time, and David rose to the rank of major. He later went on to serve as an instructor pilot with the U.S. Navy in Norfolk, in Virginia, where in the early 1980s he was the victim of a tragic accident.

It occurred one day while accompanying a cadet in a jet for a simulated dive. The cadet apparently froze mid-flight, and when David attempted to eject from the out-of-control aircraft, the canopy, or roof, did not break away, and he was pushed through it. David spent the next ninety days in intensive care and was later discharged from the military with 90 percent disability. The cadet, unfortunately, did not survive. David, after recovering, went on to become a lobbyist in Washington for Northrop Jet Company.[5]

CHAPTER 2

BOB JONES UNIVERSITY

It was decided long before I graduated high school that I would attend Bob Jones University in Greenville, South Carolina. This was my parents' decision, not mine, as it usually went in those days.

Many people outside of the religious world may not have heard of Bob Jones University, but those who have certainly know the school's strict reputation. I knew that I really didn't want to go there, and had I been given a say in the matter I likely would have attended Ohio State instead. But in 1964, no one would ever go against their parents' wishes. At least no one from Mansfield, Ohio who was brought up attending church several times a week.

Bob Jones University was technically a non-denominational school, but it was primarily Southern Baptist in orientation. My parents were drawn to this particular school because my aunt and uncle belonged to Grace Brethren Church, which is also similar to Southern Baptist, if not more conservative, and the pastor there had attended Bob Jones.

My college experience bore many similarities to the military in its emphasis on discipline, regimentation, and punishment.

Among the rules of Bob Jones University: No dating without a chaperone. No skirts above the knee. No talking to a woman past 6:00 p.m., other than to say hello. Absolutely no alcohol – even certain sodas were off limits. Curfew was strictly observed at 10:00 p.m. with prayer meetings from 10:30

to 11:00 p.m. every night. And you better get right to sleep because Monday through Friday the morning bell rang at 6:55 a.m. and you were expected to be out of bed with your feet on the floor at 6:56 a.m. The hall monitor would check rooms to make sure you were up on time. You could hear the doors open and shut in rapid succession as he came down the hall to make sure you were out of the rack.

Dinner was served at 6:00 p.m. Every student was required to eat dinner in the dining hall. The men were required to dress in white shirts, ties, and coats. There were twenty-two people assigned to each table, and roll was taken at each meal. If you were a no-show, an upperclassman would fill out a slip and turn it into the discipline committee. The following week, you would attend a discipline class and explain why you were a no-show. If your reason wasn't good enough, you were given demerits.

THE DEMERIT SYSTEM

When students registered for classes, everyone was required to leave one period free for the demerit committee. While you might think that the young men of Bob Jones University would be lenient toward each other out of comradery, it was usually quite the opposite. Some students adopted the responsibility of handing out demerits with religious fervor — you may even call them radical. So not only did you have the administration constantly watching over your shoulder, you also had to conduct yourself properly in the company of your own classmates.

Each student was allowed 150 demerits per semester — after that, you were subject to being "shipped," or kicked out of school. Each offense carried a different number of demerits. If a student was caught cheating, that was considered a major offense for which he would receive many demerits. Most of the demerits handed out were for seemingly minor offenses like listening to rock n' roll music. I say *seemingly* minor, because playing a band as "barbarian" as, say, The Beatles, could land you seventy-five demerits, or half of your allowance. The music of Peter, Paul and Mary was approved, but even that was frowned upon if listened to too often. I received only minor demerits during my years at Bob Jones, mostly for not completing my dorm room responsibilities. For example, a hall monitor would write me up for not picking up all of the empty Coke bottles in my room. Coca-Cola was allowed, but you had better not get caught sipping on something as unseemly as a Mountain Dew soda, as the name alluded to moonshine. It goes without saying, getting caught with actual alcohol would have gotten one shipped with no questions, end of story. The same went for stealing. Two weeks into my freshman year, it came to the school's attention that someone had been stealing.

In hopes of catching the thief, the hall monitors planted money that had been dusted with a special powder that would show up under ultraviolet light. At 10:30 p.m. one Sunday evening, everyone from my dorm was ushered into the hall. The monitor held out an ultraviolet light and ordered everyone to extend their hands. I remember being scared to death that something would show up on my hands, even though I wasn't the culprit. Practices such as these created a culture of fear and paranoia at Bob Jones University, even among the most straitlaced students.

The thief was eventually caught, though I did not witness his capture. There were four dorms in all, and he did not reside in mine.

The summer after my freshman year, I went home to Mansfield, Ohio. One afternoon, some friends and I went to Park Lanes Bowling Alley, an establishment known to serve liquor, as many bowling alleys do. When I got back to school in September, there was a note in my mailbox from Dr. Dean Lively, Dean of Men, instructing me to report to him upon my arrival. At the time I had no idea why but knew it couldn't be good. I did what I was told and went to see him.

He informed me that an unidentified schoolmate of mine saw me enter Park Lanes. Although I did not consume any alcohol that evening, and the dean believed me, simply being in the presence of it was reason enough to get me in trouble. Well, almost.

Dr. Dean Lively was an older guy, and he was intimidating as all hell. Despite his small stature, his demeanor and his direct methods had earned him quite a reputation. He said, "It was reported that on *X date* you frequented Park Lanes, which I understand is a bowling alley that serves alcohol. Is that so?" I responded, "Yes, sir. I bowled there." He responded, "Don't you understand what a bad testimony that is, and a reflection on you and the school? I appreciate your honesty, and I'm taking no further action at this time. But don't let it happen again." I responded with, "Yes, sir."

At Bob Jones University, this was considered catching a break, and I knew better than to say anything more.

ACCOUNTING

I wasn't sure what I wanted to major in when I began my college career, but I did know that I wanted to be at Bob Jones University for the shortest possible amount of time. I found an "out" by studying chemistry with the objective of becoming a pharmacist — a course of study not offered at Bob Jones University. I figured with this plan I would only need to spend at most a year at this establishment, and then I could transfer to somewhere more desirable to complete my degree. However, it wasn't long before my plan changed.

Two of my three roommates were accounting majors and through them I was introduced to the world of accounting. I instantly fell in love with its rules and procedures, and found that its processes, whether it was cost accounting or taxation, truly aligned with who I was as a person. Whereas my chemistry coursework had felt like a foreign language, accounting came much more naturally to me. Switching to accounting would mean three more years at Bob Jones University, and, from what I'd heard, the program was extremely difficult. I'd really have to buckle down to be a successful accounting major, but ultimately, I decided the benefits outweighed the costs if it meant I would actually understand and enjoy my work.

When I arrived back at school for my sophomore year, I changed my major. I had been warned that the second exam in the accounting program was a ball-buster, and everything was graded on the curve. Of those taking the exam, 90 percent scored 50 percent or less. The school posted the scores, but they were listed by social security number instead of by name to spare anyone embarrassment, or in my case, notoriety.

You see, I was somewhat of a nerd. The summer before my sophomore year, I got an accounting textbook and studied it at the library every day. In the fall, I took the exam and blew everyone away by scoring 100 percent. The next highest score was 80 percent. No one else had ever done this. But due to my extensive over-preparation, I had given myself an unfair advantage, and subsequently sealed my position in the program and my fate. I ended up staying at Bob Jones University for four very long years.

SECURITY

I had two jobs while at Bob Jones University. These allowed me to save enough money to buy my longtime girlfriend, Barbara, an engagement ring, which we'll get to shortly.

I started my first job during my junior year as part of the school's security force. My shift was from 2:00 a.m. to 6:00 a.m., five nights a week which, you can imagine, was a pretty rough schedule for a college student. My responsibilities included keying several boxes for insurance purposes, as the school's insurance company required certain places on campus to be monitored on a regimented basis for building safety and in case of fire or theft. I was assigned a route to follow with ten stops every hour. My area was the art museum, which at the time was the second largest religious art museum in the world. I had to repeat my ten stops every hour, though the route only took me twenty minutes. I made use of an alarm clock to fit some sleep into my schedule. I'd do my first watch from 2:00 to 2:20 a.m., then sleep from 2:20 to 3:00 a.m., wake up and do my next shift, sleep for another 40 minutes, and repeat this pattern until my shift was over. This job quickly proved to be too much of a drain, as I had to be up by 7:00 a.m. for a full day of classes and studying. The inconsistent sleep schedule had me feeling like a zombie; I lasted just six months.

Richland Screw Machine Shop

In addition to the on-campus jobs I held at Bob Jones University, I also had a couple of off-campus jobs that I worked on my summer breaks. One of them was for my uncle's screw machine shop. I am not at all mechanically inclined, so my experience during these summers was not much fun. I found working in the shop to be tedious, boring, and totally abysmal. From milling machines to lathes, to threading machines and having to use oil to keep the machine cool while it was in operation, the shop was an oily mess full of dangerous scraps of steel. It only further entrenched into my brain that this environment was not for me, and not what I wanted for my future. It showed me what the real value of an education could do to develop a future, and it gave me further evidence that I was on the right path by pursuing a college education.

Thermo Disc

Thermo Disc manufactured thermostats, and my summer job there was to deliver parts to the assembly line and to ensure that there were no slowdowns due to missing parts. My boss during the two summers I worked there was none other than my future father-in-law, Wilbur Wade. He was a real jock and quite often carried a scowl on his face. I am fairly certain this scowl was directed toward me as a means of intimidation and a warning to my mind P's and Q's since I was dating his daughter. Although this job was easier than working in the screw machine shop, it inspired the same thoughts: get your college education. The fact that I survived those two summers working for my soon-to-be father-in-law virtually unscathed was a real accomplishment.

THE WAX CREW

I began on the wax crew my senior year. Ninety percent of the flooring on campus was lightly colored vinyl asbestos tile (VAT), upon which 3,000 students would stomp on each day, leaving black scuff marks on the floors. Needless to say, the wax crew had a big job to do each night. My shift was from 11:00 p.m. to 2:00 a.m. – still prohibiting me from getting a full eight hours, but much better than my previous job's hours. Everyone on the crew had a partner with whom they shared certain areas of responsibility. My partner was Donald Carbaugh, who became a good friend.

Three weeks before graduation, Carbaugh and I did something fairly stupid, looking back. It would prove to be my one rebellion at Bob Jones University and to this day, I am still not completely sure what our motivation was. I was so close to graduation, and the prank we pulled could have jeopardized everything.

I guess after the nearly four years I'd let Bob Jones University beat me down, I just couldn't resist the urge to pull one over on the administration and watch them try to catch me.

Carbaugh and I planned our prank for weeks and we trusted each other to both keep our mouths shut, no matter what happened.

Our plan, though juvenile in nature, was thorough and calculated. There was a large fountain at the entrance of the school campus, just behind the security gate. This fountain was seen as the focal point of the campus, which was otherwise rather clean, plain, and sterile looking. It was certainly one of the only features on campus that the school had invested a significant amount of money into purely for aesthetic purposes.

We knew the fountain turned off at a certain time each evening and turned back on each morning. We bought the largest box of laundry powder we could find and hid it. Then sometime after curfew, when the fountain was off, we poured the entire box of soap into it. The next morning when the fountain turned on, it exploded with soap suds, even larger and more magnificent than anything we could have anticipated. The foamy white suds spilled out over the sides and front of the fountain, stretching across the entire courtyard, and standing taller than a person. It was our masterpiece.

The whole school saw it, as did anyone driving by the main entrance. School officials worked quickly to remove the mess and the suds were cleaned up by around 9:00 p.m. the next night, but not before causing a tremendous amount of scuttlebutt. The Dean of Men, Dr. Dean Lively, was fit to be tied. He summoned all members of the wax crew, knowing our late-night schedules made us the most likely culprits. Naturally, I was nervous, though only my partner and I knew what happened. Lively started by laying guilt on the group to see if anyone would come forward. I wasn't standing next to Carbaugh at the time, but I knew neither one of us was talking.

The dean got nowhere with his initial interrogation, so he decided to separate the wax crew. One by one he called us into a conference room. Keep in mind that I am not a likely suspect, given my spotless record. The only blemish would have been my bowling alley visit two years prior, but in those two years I had established a solid reputation. The administration would have been flabbergasted if I were involved. When it was my turn, Dr. Dean Lively said, "I only have two questions to ask you. Did you create this dilemma of soap in the fountain?" I said, "No, sir." He continued, "Do you know who did it?" I said, "No, sir," to which he responded, "You're dismissed."

Outwardly I appeared calm, but on the inside was a wreck, asking myself, "Why did you do this? How stupid can you be?" At this point I was a senior, only three weeks away from graduation, and would have had a big problem if I were caught. Although I trusted him, I allowed myself to momentarily agonize over whether Carbaugh would crack under Lively's pressure, especially since his résumé was more tainted than mine and may have warranted a harsher grilling. Fortunately, he was strong and did not fold. Because the administration couldn't pin the event on anyone, there were no repercussions. It was a miracle, but we got away with it.

MARRIAGE

I met my future wife, Barbara, when I was in the eighth grade and she was in the seventh grade at Johnny Appleseed Junior High School. Our lockers were very near each other, and I was attracted to her the first day I saw her. I can remember carrying her clarinet case, which probably looked funny because at that time she was taller than I was.

During our high school days, we were almost inseparable. We went to the same church, had the same friends, and were what I would consider a very stable couple. Barbara was a jock and could regularly beat me at just about anything athletic. To this day, she continues to beat me at bowling, golf, and most activities of the sort. I've always been amazed by her abilities.

Upon my graduation from high school, I was off to Greenville, South Carolina to attend Bob Jones University. Barbara was entering her senior year of high school. It was the first time we'd ever been apart for any significant amount of time. For the next three-and-a-half years we were separated by distance, but the romance between the two of us continued to grow. During Christmas break in 1966 at her home, in front of the Christmas tree, with only the two of us there, I asked her if she would marry me. The answer, fortunately, was yes. We married in Mansfield one year and one day later, on December 23, 1967. I remember it snowed that day. We honeymooned in the Poconos, then drove back to Bob Jones University in time for me to begin the final semester of my senior year.

Barbara found a job working at Walgreens, and we moved into a nice little apartment owned by one of the faculty members of the university. It became our home away from home.

Barbara was only on campus a minimal amount. At a conservative school such as Bob Jones University, it was not unusual for women to be asked to kneel in order to confirm that their skirts were the proper length, which is to say, to the knee. This was during the miniskirt craze and my wife, with her athletic legs and lovely figure, wore miniskirts often. The likelihood of her getting me into hot water was basically a given.

Approximately one month after we had been married, we received a serious phone call from my mother. This would affect both of us, especially me. She called to let me know that my father, at the age of thirty-nine, had died of a heart attack. Needless to say, this turned our lives upside down.

My relationship with my dad was what I considered fairly superficial. He worked all the time as an engineer at Westinghouse. In his mid-thirties, he changed careers to become a high school teacher, taking a two-thirds cut in his pay to do so. As a money-motivated accounting major, this was something I could never understand. Frankly, I thought he was nuts. But my father said he felt it was his calling from the Lord, and I realize that some people feel they're being told by a higher power that they have a greater purpose to serve in life. And, regardless of whether I can personally relate, who am I to argue that?

Although I never felt particularly close with my father, his death left a void in my life. Up until that point, he had always been there to help me make important decisions. When he died, I lost my mentor. I felt alone, especially seeing as I was just five months from graduating college and about to enter the so-called "real world." Fortunately, I had been offered a great job before he died. It gave me some comfort to know that my father died knowing I had a successful career path lined up, although the war would soon change my course.

GRADUATION AND DEAN LAUTENBACH

I was part of a graduating class of about 300 at Bob Jones University. Of the 100 who started as freshmen with a major in accounting, only nineteen made it to the finish line to earn a Bachelor of Science with a major in accounting. I was proud of my accomplishments thus far.

Upon graduation I had three offers from the big eight accounting firms, which included Price Waterhouse, Ernst and Ernst, and Arthur Andersen. I sought the advice of the Dean of the School of Business, Lawrence Lautenbach, to help make my decision. Lautenbach was a formidable looking gentleman — big, bald-headed, and gruff. He was always somewhat aloof, but if he thought you were good enough, he would take you under his wing. This is what he did with me, and after my father passed away he took on an even more father-like role in my life. I would have followed his direction wherever he told me to go. So, when he indicated that I should seriously consider going with Price Waterhouse, I didn't think twice. That was all he needed to say.

Lautenbach was a controversial figure at Bob Jones University. He was a retired businessman who had created a niche for us oddball accounting majors who would become ardently welcomed by the big eight accounting firms. However, senior management of the school saw him as standing for things they considered detrimental to the good of the school. If you were an accounting major, you were looked down upon because your major stood for profit in business when you were supposed to be out saving souls. But Lautenbach's ability to place graduates in the major accounting firms gave him a cult-like following among us, and we were treated very well in the accounting world.

I am convinced his guidance and insight is what helped me land my dream job in accounting.

CHAPTER 3

PRICE WATERHOUSE

Toward the end of my senior year at Bob Jones University, I landed an interview with Price Waterhouse for a position in Columbus, Ohio. The interview process had been rigorous, lasting all day. After lunch, one of the bigwigs asked me how I thought things were going. I told him it was the place I wanted to be, and he said something like, "Well that's good to hear, because we want you."

After graduation I accepted a position and began working on June 1, 1968. My annual salary in 1968 was $8,300. Over fifty years later, at the time this book is being written, that sum sounds pretty ridiculous, but it was a fair market rate at the time. And it felt like a lot of money to someone of my background, fresh out of school, who was used to living a fairly simple lifestyle.

My initial assignment was a thirty-day class to indoctrinate me into the Price Waterhouse way of doing things. Out of the twenty new hires, I was the oddball of the group because I had graduated from Bob Jones University.

Don't get me wrong, the fact that I earned an accounting degree from a reputable university put me on the map. The big eight accounting firms held graduates of Bob Jones in high regard. The oddball reputation was due to the fact that students at Bob Jones University don't smoke, don't drink, and don't carouse, and that was simply uncharacteristic of a young man in the business world at the time. A productive day's work was its own reward for the graduates of Bob Jones. While rule following was not a hardship for me, I was teased for it. Thankfully, the teasing was good-natured. It didn't bother me that I was not part of the after-work happy hour. I had a wife at home and did not see the necessity of such behavior. I did not drink and did not think highly of those who did so, especially those who went out just to get drunk. So perhaps I was a bit judgmental, too.

The first public accounting project I was assigned by Price Waterhouse was an audit for Cooper Tires, a client based in Mount Vernon, Ohio. Mount Vernon was thirty miles from Mansfield, where Barbara and I were living with my mother, now a widow. This arrangement provided my mother with company and was also the cheapest option for Barbara and me.

I showed up at the Cooper Tires office in Mount Vernon every weekday through August, but my time on the job was cut short. After years of knowing it could come at any moment, I received my draft notice from Uncle Sam a week before Labor Day in 1968. The letter indicated that I was to be at the enlistment office on September 16, 1968. Three weeks was all the notice I got.

F. BRUCE LAUER

Bruce Lauer

PERSONAL DATA
Home of Record: Mansfield, OH
Date of Birth: Sunday, July 21, 1946

MILITARY DATA
Service: Army of the United States
Rank/Title: Specialist Fifth Class
ID No: US51885612
MOS: 73F
Unit: Americal Division

THE DRAFT

When I received my draft notice in the mail, it felt like I'd been punched in the stomach. It was as if all the air rushed out of my body, making it difficult to catch my breath.

From the day I turned eighteen, I knew there was a possibility I would come home to find that letter in the mailbox, but it was always in the back of my mind. To put things in perspective of how little thought I gave to being drafted, Barbara and I had never even discussed the possibility with each other. We never talked about what we would do if I had to leave for Vietnam. In hindsight, maybe we both just wanted to delay that painful conversation as long as we could.

When I told Price Waterhouse, they said they wouldn't be able to give me any accounts until I returned and essentially told me, "Good luck. We'll see you in two years." It was nice to have time before leaving to be with family and to get our affairs in order, but it also gave me too much time to think, to play through all the "what ifs" in my head and ruminate the many potential scenarios of my own demise. Truthfully, the distraction of work during that time would not have been unwelcome.

It really wasn't until after I graduated from Bob Jones University that I began to understand the momentum of the Vietnam conflict. I still didn't know everything, but I was aware that by that point, we had virtually no chance of winning. I'd also become more attuned to the fact that so many Americans opposed the war vehemently. So, my attitude toward Vietnam was less than optimistic, to say the least. While, of course, I was proud to serve my country, I'd be lying if I told you I was particularly excited about it. To be candid, I was scared shitless.

This was a time in my life when I could have really used my father's advice. I could have used someone to tell me that I had options. I figured my choices were either to go to Vietnam or flee to Canada, and as I mentioned before, the latter option was never on the table. I suppose I could have also attended graduate school and continued to defer, but that would only buy me two guaranteed years. Plus, I knew Barbara and I would soon want to start a family, and it would have been much more difficult to leave if we had already had a child.

Had my father still been with us, I imagine he would have opened up the possibility of attending Officer Candidate School (OCS), a program open to college graduates that fast-tracked one's route to becoming an officer — a much better position to have in Vietnam than coming in as an enlisted man. Although I'd heard of OCS, I didn't know much about it, and I had no one there to discuss the pros and cons of pursuing that path. I didn't even know I would be eligible, much less how to apply. I am not sure whether things would have turned out better or worse for me had I taken the OCS path, but the point is, I had really nobody there to encourage me one way or the other.

I was drafted on September 16, 1968, a Monday. I will never forget that fateful day. It began with an early morning ride with Barbara, who dropped me off at the Farmers Bank Building in downtown Mansfield, Ohio. In a town as small as Mansfield, there was no official recruiting station. The bank building was a central location from which my fellow recruits and I could board a military bus to Fort Hays in Columbus. Barbara and I took the brand new 1968 Pontiac LeMans that I had recently purchased so that I could be there at the designated time — 5:30 a.m. It was very difficult leaving my wife of nine months, knowing I would not see her again until Thanksgiving after I'd completed basic training. Nevertheless, we said our goodbyes, and I boarded a bus full of strangers, twenty-five other guys with whom I was entering into an uncharted, unpredictable world that would mold many aspects of my life from that day on.

At Fort Hays, I was to take the oath indicating that I was in concert with joining the U.S. Army. I had no objection, I was proud to serve my country, but that didn't mean I wasn't nervous. There were forty or so of us in one room at Fort Hays waiting to be inducted. A captain came in to give us the oath of enlistment. He was a young guy, maybe in his early thirties, and he was very serious. As the captain was giving preliminary instructions of what was about to happen to each of us, all of a sudden, one guy said in a loud voice, "Captain, I am not going to take the oath." There was complete silence. It was evident that this was not the first time the captain had encountered a malcontent who had no interest in becoming part of Uncle Sam's Army. The captain asked, "Are you sure you want to do this?" And the guy said, "Yes," without pause. There were military police (MPs) in the room. After being questioned for two or three minutes, the malcontent was escorted away without incident. He was the only one of the forty who indicated that he was not willing to be part of this endeavor. The rest of us were then given the oath and inducted into the U.S. Army.

I believed, and still believe, that everyone has a responsibility to serve their country. I felt disdain for this guy who would not take the oath. I felt it was not only un-American, but also selfish and cowardly.

My next stop was the airport in Columbus, Ohio where I boarded a plane bound for Columbia, South Carolina. From there, I boarded an Army bus and was driven to Fort Jackson, South Carolina. Coincidentally, I was not far from Bob Jones University.

Basic Training

September in Fort Jackson, South Carolina, is hot, muggy, and nearly unbearable. This is where we were taken to begin basic training, which lasted eight weeks. I have many memories of that eight-week period, most of which are not good.

With our duffle bags, we piled into a brown Army bus to be driven to our assigned units. During this process, drill sergeants in Smokey-the-Bear hats — the ones with large, circular, flat brims — yelled at us using very graphic four-letter words. Harassment and intimidation — those were the calling cards for the next eight weeks.

We were assigned to squads — A, B, C, etc. Every morning, we stood at attention in the pitch black for reveille and were subjected to the whims of the drill sergeant. One requirement was to give a status, or standing, of our unit. My squad included a Private Bosco who was there on the first day, but then disappeared. From the second day on through to the last day, eight weeks later, our morning report read, "Private Bosco AWOL." AWOL stood for "absent without leave." To the best of my knowledge, he was never caught. This young man, in my mind, committed an even more cowardly act than the guy who'd declined to take the oath at Fort Hays. This feeling was multiplied after a few days at basic training when I truly began to understand what these men ran away from, while the rest of us struggled to get through it.

Reveille was at 6:00 a.m., and we learned very quickly to run to the middle whenever a formation was called — head down, no eye contact. That way, individuals would perhaps have less of a chance of being selected for some type of extra duty, which could be anything from kitchen police (KP) to guard duty, or anything else that the cadre figured might ruin your day.

Hazing

The bus ride from Mansfield, Ohio to Columbus was fairly short, and the stay at Fort Hays kept us there until mid-evening, at which time we were taken to the Columbus airport. For some reason our plane was delayed, and since we did not leave until midnight, we arrived at Fort Jackson at about 3:00 a.m. Upon our arrival, we were escorted by one of the cadre into a barracks and told to grab any bunk bed that was not being used.

We were exhausted, and it seemed like only moments since we had fallen asleep before some Army personnel was yelling at the top of his lungs for us to get up, get outside, and get into formation. Now mind you, it's 6:00 a.m., and we've only had approximately three hours of sleep. Then suddenly, we were being harassed by a sergeant who seemed to enjoy getting in our faces and telling us what lowly animals we were, warning us that if we didn't get moving quickly to the mess hall, breakfast would be over and we would go without.

My first day in the Army was confusing, intimidating, and frightening, but it went by fast. After we finished breakfast, we were taken to the supply building to receive our issue of Army clothing. The various pieces of gear and garments we received were primarily olive green, except for khakis for special occasions. We stashed all of the clothing, boots, and whatever else they gave us in duffel bags, which were our constant companions and were getting heavier by the moment.

As we were marched back to the barracks, we were told to change out of our civilian clothing, which we would no longer need. We were given a choice: either send them back or throw them in the trash can. Most of us simply took our civilian clothing and trashed it, then put on our green Army fatigues and boots and formed up to go to the mess hall for lunch. The only thing of value I kept was my wedding ring. I had left my watch at home, for fear that I would lose it or have it taken from me.

As we approached the mess hall, I noticed that there was a long set of monkey bars in front of the building. I learned, to my dismay, these monkey bars were part of the dining procedure. Before sitting down for a meal, whether it was breakfast, lunch or dinner, everyone had to attempt to swing across them as quickly as possible without dropping to the ground before reaching the end. I must confess that I was out of shape when I arrived and had very soft hands, because I was an accountant. On my first attempt, I could not make it from the beginning of the monkey bars to the end; part of the way through, I fell to the ground.

When I fell, I met Corporal DeLucia, who was in my face calling me every four-letter word on earth — many of which I had never even heard, being the sheltered, young Christian man that I was. He shouted that my wife could handle those monkey bars better than I could, which truthfully, may have been correct given the athletic edge she has on me to this day. But that aside, this was pure harassment to the highest degree. The obvious objective was to make me mad and realize that this harassment was going to take place before every meal until I improved. It was clear that Corporal DeLucia was going to be in my face until I learned to traverse those monkey bars from beginning to end in a quick fashion without falling to the ground. It took me three days, trying three times a day, to get the hang of it — and to learn the proper technique — before I was able to cross.

I remember feeling poorly for the "big boys" in the group who had a harder time swinging their weight. Though we all had to pass a physical in order to get drafted, implying we were at least somewhat physically fit, this was not an easy task.

After lunch, we were marched over to an Army barracks that turned out to be the base hospital where we would receive the various shots and inoculations required to go through basic training and prepare us for foreign travel to Vietnam. We were told to form a straight line and remove our t-shirts. Three or four doctors came down the line, all together, each of whom were giving us a shot. They were using some sort of gun that they would put up against your shoulder, then push a button, and the medicine would penetrate your arm. It was like an assembly line, churning out hundreds of newly immunized soldiers an hour.

If you flinched or moved during the shots, you would bleed like a stuck pig. It became evident that a number of the soldiers couldn't stand the sight of blood and fainted. It was quite an ordeal. I have always been squeamish, but I managed to stay very still, having watched others go through the process in line ahead of me and observing what not to do.

The first few days in basic training kind of ran together, and before I knew it, we were into the weekend. On that first Saturday in Fort Jackson, South Carolina, we were standing in formation and our commanding officer told us that we would all be required to attend church the following day. Regardless of denomination, everybody went to the service. Coming from Bob Jones University, where we attended chapel every day and church twice on Sundays, this was of course nothing new to me. So, it wasn't much of a surprise when, after the commanding officer spoke, a second lieutenant came forward and pointed at me and at two others, indicating that we would be ushers at chapel the following morning. He also indicated that we would need to wear our khakis and to ensure that they were firmly pressed.

Unfortunately, we did not have an iron, and we were at a loss as to how we were going to get those khakis pressed to conform with the lieutenant's requirements. All of a sudden a sergeant, one of the permanent cadre members, came up to the three of us and told us that he would be willing to iron our khakis if we paid him a dollar each. My response was, "Here's your dollar. Thank you very much." The sergeant was well-built and around six feet tall, compared to my skinny, five-foot-nine frame. He was black and intimidating, and it did not occur to me to not do what he said. However, unbeknownst to me, someone else was watching as this sergeant took a buck from each of us and turned him in, because this was, in Army terms, "hazing."

The three of us ushers, who did not know each other until that day, had no inkling of the difficulty we were about to become part of, which took place after chapel the following day. This could be considered the beginning of a recurring theme — of finding myself as an innocent bystander, somehow involved in trouble that I had nothing to do with.

Once chapel was over, we were told to line up outside, and a captain addressed our unit. He stated that hazing was not to be tolerated and warned that anybody caught hazing the troops was subject to a court-martial. As he spoke, I got very nervous, for I knew where this captain was headed. Sure enough, he then asked for those who were ushers at chapel to step forward. Of course, the three of us stepped forward and the captain told us to report to him within the next thirty minutes at his office. We went immediately to his office where we waited for approximately twenty minutes before we were ushered in. We stood at attention, not knowing what the next step was.

Once we were ushered into the captain's office, I saw immediately the sergeant who had taken our dollar to press our khakis. He was standing at attention, looking straight ahead. Now mind you this sergeant was probably twenty-five years old — which was a few years older than me — and was very well-conditioned. He looked like an Army paratrooper, a position that requires the highest level of physical fitness. As a G.I. who could barely get himself across the monkey bars, he was very intimidating to me. Sizing up the situation, I realized that someone had turned this sergeant in, and the captain was looking for one of us to implicate him — and I'm thinking, "No way, it's not gonna be me." Six days into my time with the U.S. Army, I am not at all interested in creating an issue that might be harmful to me later on.

So, the captain comes down and I'm the first one he looks at. He says, "Private Lauer, has anybody in this room harassed you in any way, shape, or form?" My immediate answer was, "No sir."

The captain then moved on to the other two and their responses were the same as mine. At that time, the captain said, "Thank you very much. You're dismissed."

Fortunately, that was the end of the story, and I did not see that sergeant or captain again during my eight weeks in Fort Jackson, nor did I discuss this situation with the other two ushers.

PRIVATE PHILLIPS

During that initial eight weeks at basic training, it was hot, muggy, and the physical training was onerous. However, at the end of eight weeks I was in the best physical shape I had ever been in my entire life. Let's just say that when I finally got home to Barbara for Thanksgiving, she was pretty impressed with her new and improved hunk of a husband.

Those eight weeks profoundly changed not only my physical well-being, but my mental well-being also. When you're training with others, you become one unit. Everyone works together.

I'll never forget a guy named Phillips, a private (E1) who was in our unit, who had great difficulty marching in sync. It got so bad that our drill sergeant ordered all of us to double time — meaning run twice as fast as we had been — after making Phillips break out of the formation. Then, as we were double-timing, our drill sergeant indicated the reason we were doing it was because of our buddy Phillips, who was marching out of sync. The only way the drill sergeant knew how to fix that was to get us, his buddies, upset at him. In addition to the fact that we were now running at twice the speed we once were, Phillips was ordered to begin running around our unit, which meant he had to run more than twice as fast in order to go all the way around us. After doing that for about five minutes, we were ordered to halt. Phillips was put back into formation, and when we began marching once again. All of sudden, Phillips was somehow able to march in sync, and therefore ended our collective misery.

KITCHEN POLICE

All soldiers going through basic training are assigned additional duties and work details. Every detail was unpleasant in one way or another, but one of the worst details was kitchen police, or KP for short. This was one of the most difficult and unenjoyable jobs because it literally required you to be there from sunrise past sundown. The shift started at 5:00 a.m. and ended around 8:00 p.m. There were many jobs associated with KP such as peeling potatoes, washing dishes, and serving food for breakfast, lunch, and dinner. During my eight-week stint in basic training, I found myself pulling KP duty about every ten days, which means I had it five or six times.

The cooks were responsible for the running of our kitchen and the serving of meals. Because of the number of times I had the privilege of pulling KP, I got to know these folks fairly well. One incident that really sticks out in my memory took place on a Sunday afternoon. We were going to finish early when one of the cooks came to me and pointed to four boxes filled with food, and I mean tins of food, and told me to put them in his trunk. The cook looked like he may have had a third-grade education. He was a young guy, muscular, and intimidating. Because his order was not protocol, of course, I just stood there and looked at him strangely.

"Listen, I don't make enough money to feed my family and this is how I support them," he said. Not knowing what else to do, I did as I was told and put the boxes in his car. This was simply another encounter in which I found myself accidentally involved in some sort of disloyal act. While some would see taking these groceries as doing what one had to do to provide for one's family, there's no denying that it was also thievery.

Of course, I was in no position to do anything other than what I was told, and I never said the first word to anybody about this while I was in basic training. The cook would get away with this by adding fictitious names to the sign-in sheet so that it appeared he was feeding more people than he actually was.

SERGEANT FIRST CLASS HAMMER

Two days after my arrival at Fort Jackson, having been assigned to a specific unit in a specific set of barracks, a sergeant first class whose last name was Hammer came into our barracks. There was an immediate silence that fell as Sergeant First Class Hammer began to explain why he was there. The sergeant's first command to the forty of us was to know why you're here. He then asked, "Why are you here?" to which one of my comrades instantly replied, "We're here because of Vietnam." His answer was "You are 100 percent correct, and do you realize or have any inkling as to what your job will be?" There was silence as he continued, "You and your buddy next to you will be 11 Bravo."

Now 11 Bravo was a foreign sounding name, but he continued to explain, "An 11 Bravo is infantry. Do you have any inkling as to the life expectancy of an infantryman in Vietnam?" he asked. We all stared blankly, and I felt my stomach begin to turn. "Well, let me tell you," he said. "The average life expectancy of 11 Bravo in combat is twenty-two days." There was a gasp as he continued, "But I can make a difference, and by that I mean I can change your MOS (also known as Military Occupational Specialty, or job description) and you will not be an 11 Bravo." Well, that struck a chord with me because, as you'll see reading this book, I'm not exactly the bravest guy on earth. Sergeant First Class Hammer had given me some hope that when I went to Vietnam, I was not going to be an 11 Bravo and that I would live to see the end of my two-year contract.

Sergeant First Class Hammer then said, "If any of you have an interest in how I can change your MOS and keep you from being an 11 Bravo, raise your hand." Three hands raised, mine included. He met with the three of us and said the way this works is that you need to sign this paperwork that indicates that you are willing to sign up for one more year. In other words, your service would extend from two years in the Army to three. By doing that, I will guarantee that you have a different MOS than 11 Bravo, he said.

Of the job descriptions that were currently available, the one that I chose was 76Q. Or rather, there wasn't much choice involved. Hammer said, "Lauer, there's an opening in quartermaster school. I suggest you take it."

A 76Q is a supply MOS that takes you to the quartermaster school in Fort Lee, Virginia. And when it came to take it or leave it — versus the alternative of 11 Bravo — I chose QM school. An extra year in the Army sounded like a fair trade for my life. I signed the paperwork.

Later that evening, a buddy from my hometown saw me and came running. He said, "What is this that I heard, you signed up for an extra year to get a different MOS? What are you, nuts? It doesn't matter what your MOS is if you're an E4 or below in rank," he explained. "If there's some type of firefight and you happen to land in Vietnam when a unit has been wiped out, everybody E4 and below will be used, no matter what your MOS is. You'll just be used to reform that group that was wiped out, and your MOS won't mean a thing. You won't have the rank you need to make sure your MOS is actually what you end up doing. Basically, you signed up for an extra year for nothing." Understandably, that information didn't sit well with me. I thought to myself, "I have been duped, what the hell am I going to do?" I made my decision the first thing the next morning.

CHAPLAIN

Given this bad news, I went to find a chaplain who I thought would give me the best chance of getting me out of what I had signed up for; I was fortunate in that I found a chaplain who was a major. I gave him my story and through much haranguing he was able to get me out of this extra year. I felt instant relief, yet I still had a bit of trepidation.

About a week after I had been able to get out of what I'd signed up for, guess who shows up back at the barracks after dinner one evening? None other than SFC Hammer looking for, guess who, the guy who found a way out of his little scheme. Well, almost. You see, SFC Hammer received a bonus for each person he signed up and was therefore quite persuasive. Hammer was in his mid-thirties, a recruiter who was a career guy or "lifer." When he found me he stood in my face and in a menacing way he laid into me: "What the f*** are you doing? Who the f*** do you think you are? You think you can get away with this with me?"

The intimidation worked. He literally scared me into signing right back up for that extra year and taking the 76Q MOS. My decision was based on fear. I was afraid to die, whether it be on the battlefield as an 11 Bravo, or there in that moment at the hands of SFC Hammer. I felt a lump in my throat. I became resigned that this was the way it was going to be. I'd used up my last chip and did my best to move on. Although I had no idea how this decision would end up affecting me at the time, it ended up working in my favor. I suppose I should be grateful that SFC Hammer was such a skilled "negotiator."

Back at home in Ohio, my wife Barbara was living with my mother while working for Prudential Life Insurance. During basic training, I could call her once a week, and I also sent home all of my money as I did not need it where I was. The only thing she knew about the incident with SFC Hammer was that I would be in the Army for another year.

CRAPS

On the weekends we weren't allowed to go anywhere off the base. Unless we pulled KP or guard duty, we had free time. Some of the G.I.s would write letters or read books; others passed the time with something a little more enticing. This is when I first learned the game of craps.

Craps is a dice game in which the players make wagers on the outcome of a roll — or a series of rolls — of a pair of dice. On the base, I was introduced to street craps, also called simply "shooting dice." At first, I was only a bystander. Nearly all of the players were black. In that day, we called them "soul brothers." Craps is not a difficult game to understand, especially the street version. You simply roll the dice and see whatever numbers come up, the final number being the total of the two dice you rolled. It helps to know the odds. For instance, the odds of rolling four or ten are two to one. If you roll the dice and come up with a total of five or nine, the odds are seven to five. And if you roll a six or an eight, the odds are seven to six. Obviously, if the shooter rolls a four or a ten, you would naturally wager against that shooter rolling four or ten again before he rolls the inevitable seven and craps out. None of this applies in street craps because everything is even money.

In the barracks, craps was played by taking footlockers and making a U-shaped playing field. The dice were thrown up against one of the footlockers, which served as a backstop. Needless to say, whenever there was money involved in a game, it heightened the excitement. It could also create arguments, which led to the occasional fistfight. One of the more common causes of a fistfight was a dispute about how the dice came to rest after the shooter rolled. For instance, maybe one of the dice would land leaning against the footlocker, and an argument would take place on what that number really was.

I can remember watching craps for the first time on a Saturday afternoon. On this day there were five players within fifteen feet of my bunk, and I had a front row seat. It began with the inevitable chatter and placing of bets on whether or not the shooter was going to make the point or crap out. The excitement heightened as the bets got larger, then all of a sudden an argument would erupt.

In observing these games, it became readily apparent that some of the players really understood the game well and knew the odds associated with the various numbers one could roll. Conversely, other players had no clue how to place their bets. After watching people play this game every weekend, I noticed the same players were always the winners and the other players were always the losers.

I can recall one episode vividly. It took place the weekend prior to our graduation from basic training. The "usuals" showed up to play and during the course of that game, one of the players was losing badly and becoming increasingly vocal and frustrated. When he lost his last dollar playing this game — having lost around fifty dollars total — he pulled a knife and began threatening the other players to either return his money or face the consequences.

There were five players total, including the one with the knife. The other four lunged at him, pulled him to the ground and took the knife away; that's when all hell broke loose. It was four against one, so needless to say, the player with the knife was beaten pretty badly. This free-for-all created quite a ruckus, and the NCO on duty came into our barracks demanding to know what all the commotion was about. Once he saw the player who had been beaten up, he erupted in anger, and I'm sure all five players realized then that this wasn't going to end well for anyone.

The NCO called in the officer on duty, who was a second lieutenant, and he demanded some answers. The players clammed up and wouldn't give him any information that would rat on one another. The officer then turned to those of us who were watching and tried to get us to talk. Of course, no one would do so knowing that if we ratted, we would ultimately have to deal with repercussions from one or more of the players.

The second lieutenant escorted the five players to the headquarters building where, we found out later, they were questioned but again no one ratted. Despite that day's fight, the players were actually friends with one other. I suppose their silence could be viewed as a demonstration of their own code of honor.

During basic training, I learned a lot about how to stay alive and out of harm's way. I also learned the quick and exciting game of craps that, quite candidly, I love to play to this day — under the casino rules rather than the street rules that I picked up at Fort Jackson.

CHAPTER 4

ADVANCED TRAINING, FORT LEE, U.S. ARMY QUARTERMASTER SCHOOL

Upon graduation from basic training, we all received our orders for our next assignments. Of the forty-two guys in my unit, thirty-nine had orders to go to advanced infantry training. That meant they carried the MOS of 11 Bravo. Two had brothers that were already in Vietnam, so they were sent to units within the continental United States. Because of the extra year I had signed up for, I was sent to Fort Lee in Richmond, Virginia, where I would train in the quartermaster school to become a supply specialist. Our class was made up of about twenty-five guys, and the ten-week training offered a couple of benefits. If you ended up in the top two of the class, you skipped a grade with respect to your rank. Fortunately, I finished second in the class and went from an E2 to an E4, or specifically, to a specialist fourth class. After the training at Fort Lee, we were given our orders and 10 percent of our unit was headed to Vietnam. This didn't come as a surprise to me but receiving the orders did make it feel all the more real. We had a two-week leave. That is, everyone other than I had a two-week leave.

I had the unfortunate luck of pulling guard duty during the Christmas holidays while everybody else went on leave. I spent the next week "guarding" the Fort Lee facilities which, for the most part, were empty because 99 percent of the population had left to go home for the holidays.

I was allowed to call my wife, though she never came to visit me at Fort Lee during the ten weeks I was there (and I can't blame her). Many weekends, I'd hitch a ride home to see her. Because I did not have a vehicle of my own at Fort Lee, Barbara would usually meet me halfway. On one eventful weekend, she met me just outside of Athens, Ohio where Ohio University is located. It was probably about 2:00 a.m. when Barbara and I were on our way from Athens to Mansfield, and I looked in my rearview mirror to see flashing lights. A state highway patrolman pulled us over and let me know that I was speeding. As he was writing the ticket, he asked me what I did for a living. I told him I was in the U.S. Army, and his response was, "Don't tell me that because you are probably out of your area of jurisdiction and could be considered AWOL." Taking the out, I instead told him I was with Price Waterhouse.

"What is that?" he asked.

I informed him it was a public accounting firm, that it was very large, and that I worked out of the Columbus, Ohio office. Unfortunately, he was unimpressed by both my military credentials and career prowess and kept writing the ticket. Once he gave it to me, he said to follow him to the city of Athens, where I could pay the fine. This, of course, was long before the days one could pay a speeding ticket online. The fine was around $150 and, between my wife and me, we barely had enough money to scrape together to pay it.

One thing that struck me as odd about this encounter was that when the state trooper asked me where I was stationed, and I told him that I had my orders to go to Vietnam — which I thought might buy me just a warning rather than a ticket — I was sadly mistaken. That state trooper could care less that I was headed to Vietnam and was not at all sympathetic to my cause. This was yet another reminder of Americans' displeasure — or perhaps in this case, a lack of interest — in the Vietnam conflict.

After the week of pulling guard duty, I went home with my new set of orders which indicated that in March of 1969 I was to head to Fort Lewis, Washington, where I would then board a commercial jetliner to fly to Tan Son Nhut Air Force Base in Saigon, South Vietnam. After my thirty-day leave was over and I said goodbye to my wife, who I'd only been married to for fifteen months — nine of which I had been away at basic and advanced training — I flew to Fort Lewis, Washington.

CHAPTER 5

Vietnam

At Fort Lewis, we reported twice a day to hear the manifest of those individuals who had made the next flight out to end at Tan Son Nhut Air Force Base in Saigon, South Vietnam. When I heard my name, it felt as though I was being drafted all over again. A sinking feeling in my gut. An unsettling feeling of the unknown. Before Vietnam, the furthest I'd been from home was to Pike's Peak in Colorado. Now I was going to the other side of the world with very little knowledge about what awaited me.

I was somewhat surprised that our plane to Saigon was a commercial airliner with civilian stewardesses. The only difference was that every seat was occupied by military personnel, and the vast majority were Army. The eighteen-hour trip to Saigon gives one quite a bit of time to ponder what is going to happen during the next twelve months. The closer we got to Saigon, the more rampant my mind ran, playing out all the different situations of what could happen, none of which were pleasant. There were about 180 people on that plane with me. I didn't know this at the time, but I would later learn that at the time I arrived in Vietnam, more than 240 G.I.s were being killed each week. Or, in other words, more than a plane full.

As I heard the stewardess tell us over the intercom to bring our seats to the upright position and to stow away our trays, my heart began to pound. "Am I going to be shot at as soon as we land? Will the airplane be under siege?" These thoughts ran through my head, chaotically, as we descended. Not having done this before, I had no idea what to expect.

Ordinarily when a plane lands, it taxis to a gate. In this case there was no gate. We simply landed and walked down the steps to a very hot and humid afternoon in the middle of March. All of a sudden, I heard this tremendous, roaring cheer. As I looked around, I saw it was coming from a dwelling made of four poles and tin roof that housed the exact number of G.I.s that I'd just arrived with. They were waiting to get on the big bird, which they called the freedom bird, to go back to the States. Those soldiers had served their year and couldn't wait for the rest of us to get off so they could move on. It was a very unsettling feeling and not a very good way to welcome new troops to Vietnam. Although I suppose it was better than being shot at as soon as we landed, which I'd only then ruled out as a possibility.

The Combat Center

Upon arrival at Tan Son Nhut Air Force Base, we were immediately taken to the Combat Center to be processed into the Republic of South Vietnam. This is where you find out, after a few days of indoctrination, your initial permanent assignment. It was the usual hurry up and wait. We were given the various garb that we would need for the next twelve months, not unlike what we received in basic training. From green underwear to green t-shirts and boots, this was our new day-to-day uniform. The next step was finding out which unit we were going to be permanently assigned to. Like at Fort Lewis, a manifest was read twice a day, and we would all go listen for our names to learn what unit we were going to. Where we met for the manifest briefing there was a very large map of South Vietnam; as a newbie, I could not pronounce very many of the city names on the map.

The average tenure at the Combat Center was about three days. On my third day there, when I still hadn't heard my name called, I was a bit perplexed. Even the sergeant in charge of the Combat Center said, "Lauer, I have no idea why you're still here."

As my luck would have it, although 99 percent of the other incoming personnel found their permanent assignment within seventy-two hours, I would be at the Combat Center for nearly a week.

SHIT BURNING

Other than waiting to learn about permanent assignments, there are two main things one does at the Combat Center.

First, you learn about the many different ways the North Vietnamese, or Vietcong, could kill you. It was quite interesting, and downright scary, to hear the different ways our opponent could inflict pain, or much worse, upon us. From an ambush in the dense brush, to the unassuming yet instantly lethal claymore mine, to a stray piece of shrapnel spiraling through the air, the threat of danger, it seemed, was ever-present.

And then there was the second thing — work. While we were waiting for those final assignments, we went through a regimen that included many different details, similar to those at basic training. We had to make sure that whatever our assignment was, it was carried out to the fullest extent possible. None of them were fun, but the worst detail one could get was filling sandbags. Filling sandbag after sandbag created blisters on our hands and made us miserable in the intense heat. The next worst thing we could be assigned to was KP because of the grueling hours and a slew of other reasons we've already discussed. Another potential detail was picking up cigarette butts, which really bothered me since I didn't smoke, and had a real problem going around picking up other people's butts.

While I dabbled in just about every detail possible at some point or another, my detail for six days at the Combat Center was none other than the shit burning detail. Unfortunately, it's no more glamorous than it sounds. There were approximately eight different locations in which there was a latrine or outhouse, and my responsibility was to make sure that — three times a day — the latrines or outhouses were cleaned, and the excretion burned.

Each morning I would go to the Combat Center headquarters and there would be assembled what we called "day hires." These were Vietnamese who were looking for work as day laborers. I would pick out six of these individuals and they would accompany me to, for lack of a better term, burn shit. Usually the outhouses were elevated, and the excrement was collected in fifty-five-gallon drums cut in half. Most people know what an outhouse is even if they have never used one. Consider yourself lucky if that's the case. Either way, the foul odor that was emitted from these fifty-five-gallon drums was indescribable. The stench was absolutely horrible. My responsibility was to push — or in other words, yell at — the Vietnamese who were under my direction to remove the fifty-five gallon drum from the latrine and, by grabbing a handle on each side, drag it some quarter-mile away to the dump. There, we would pour diesel fuel into the drum and light it up by throwing a match on top, effectively setting the shit aflame.

With the smell of the drums already putrid, you can imagine that adding diesel fuel and burning it made things infinitely worse. If that diesel fuel splashed on our clothing, that smell alone was nauseating. I had to keep close contact with the South Vietnamese laborers because this was an ugly assignment, and they would do everything within their power to disappear rather than stick it out and get paid at the end of the day. Those South Vietnamese who were chosen for this assignment were paid one hundred piasters for the day, which was equivalent to one U.S. dollar.

One of the potentially deadly issues those of us handling the latrines had to deal with was "fragging." Fragging was a term used by the enlisted personnel to describe the dangerous activity of hurling a shrapnel grenade at someone while they were sitting on the "throne." Each latrine location had at least two and sometimes four holes, it was considered to be an excellent place to punish someone, since they were vulnerable and couldn't see anyone coming. The latrines were not monitored, so it was unlikely that the culprit would get caught unless he bragged to someone who then turned him in.

During my short stay in the Combat Center, we had one fragging incident that I was aware of. One of our enlisted men evidently had great difficulty with his commanding officer. One night when the commanding officer went to visit the throne and was seated with his pants down, this enlisted individual rolled a fragging grenade into the stall and severely maimed the officer. Needless to say, this incident sent shivers down my spine. When I saw the destruction the following morning — the blood all over the partitions — it really hit home for the first time since leaving the United States that the Vietnamese were not the only threat to my well-being. Being in a war zone can lead one to do unimaginable things, even to our own side. I realized that I had to be continually aware of my surroundings because everybody had a weapon, and if the moment struck them, they might use it on me.

From that day on to the end of my tour in South Vietnam, I was always on edge, always looking over my shoulder.

Beyond simply trying to stay alive, I spent those six long days at the Combat Center constantly wondering what my permanent assignment would be. Could it possibly be any worse than what I was already going through? And if so, could I handle it?

Little did I know, I was about to be given a permanent assignment that would rival any that were available in Uncle Sam's Army in the Republic of South Vietnam — in a good way.

CHAPEL IN A WAR ZONE

One of the days I spent at the Combat Center happened to be Palm Sunday. I vividly remember visiting the chapel that day, probably because it would be the only time in my more than eleven months in Vietnam that I would attend a church service. This was primarily because there weren't any chapels available to me at my next post. Coming from Bob Jones University, where I went to church every day — sometimes more than once a day — this was a major lifestyle change for me. But it did not bother me, as I always felt secure in my relationship with God and my faith, and I didn't necessarily need a church to pray.

I remember that while the service that day was very watered down compared to what I was used to, the chaplain focused on the theme of eternity. It was eerily fitting on this bright and sunny day as we prepared to embark on an unknown journey.

What stood out to me most while observing this service was the feeling of desperation in the air. Everyone there knew they may not make it back, and therefore, were trying to make it right with God. I would guess that most of the guys there that day had never darkened the door of a church, yet when confronted with the idea of their own death, they suddenly became God fearing.

SEVEN DAYS

On my seventh day at the Combat Center, when my shit burning detail had really begun to wear me down, the sergeant in charge came looking for me.

"Lauer, you're to go to personnel and that's probably good because they've selected you for a specific job," he said. "But I have no idea what it is."

Relieved, yet still somewhat hesitant, I grabbed a ride to the personnel office, and when I went in the sergeant behind the counter said, "Lauer, you are going to the Americal Division NCO/EM Open Mess system." I asked, "What's that?"

He replied, "Chu Lai is in the northern I Corps. The closest big city is Da Nang. There is a large division called the Americal Division. You are being assigned to the club system." He explained, "The club system runs clubs for the enlisted men and, because of your accounting degree and the fact that you were with Price Waterhouse, you have been selected to run the day to day operations. You've probably really lucked out with this job." That was my first glimpse of what would become my job for the ensuing eleven months and nineteen days in South Vietnam. From the way the sergeant presented it, it sounded like the rough couple of months I'd had between basic training and the Combat Center may have been worth the pain.

Me and Mr. Chun, the project manager who was in charge of building the Americal Division's clubs. *Chu Lai, August 1969.*

The sign at the entrance to the Americal Division club system offices. *Chu Lai, August 1969.*

Sgt. Spencer and Sgt. Freeze, the lead scavenger for the club system, with a Ford 150. *Chu Lai, August 1969.*

Pallets of Carling Black Label beer, each containing 1920 cans, stacked in front of a club system warehouse. *Chu Lai, August 1969.*

Two Filipino bookkeepers, Nestor and Cesar, who worked within the Americal Division club system. These were very reliable men. *Chu Lai, August 1969.*

Me posing for a photo with a Ford 150.
Chu Lai, August 1969.

Vietnamese workers along with soldiers enjoying lunch to celebrate Tết, the most important holiday in Vietnamese culture. It was the club system's way of saying thank you. *Chu Lai, February 1970.*

My wife Barbara, during our R&R trip to Oahu, Hawaii, demonstrating the halfway-around-the-world distance between Ohio and Vietnam. *Oahu, January 1970.*

Bob Hope performing a Christmas special for soldiers in the Americal Division. *Chu Lai, December 1969.*

Me, seated at Sgt. Gardner's desk inside his air-conditioned, wood-paneled office — the nicest office in the Americal Division. *Chu Lai, January 1970.*

The water tank that served as our shower in the club system. Non-potable water ran through a garden hose. *Chu Lai, June 1969.*

Mr. Kim, a very smart man who was responsible for the maintenance of the club system's 202 slot machines. *Chu Lai, June 1969.*

Me in front of a hooch, also known as the sleeping quarters, adorned with the Americal Division insignia. *Chu Lai, May 1969.*

I first saw this ivory boat in a merchant's window during a supply run to Saigon with Mr. Chun. Two weeks later, Mr. Chun gifted it to me. It's still displayed in a bookcase in my home. *Chu Lai, November 1969.*

Sgt. Leatherwood, who became my boss after Sgt. Gardner, driving a salvage vehicle. Chu Lai, November 1969.

Vietnamese workers loading a vehicle with hard liquor to take to a club. *Chu Lai, September 1969.*

Two daily hires washing a car. They were paid a hundred piasters a day, the equivalent of one American $1. *Chu Lai, November 1969.*

The nightly crew getting together for dinner, which was usually prepared on an outdoor grill. *Chu Lai, September 1969.*

CHAPTER 6

AMERICAL DIVISION

The Americal Division of the United States Army was formed on May 24, 1942 on the island of New Caledonia. It was created during the emergency immediately following Pearl Harbor. The United States had hurriedly sent three individual regiments to defend New Caledonia against another potential Japanese attack. It was the only division formed outside of the United States during World War II and would later carry the same distinction during the Vietnam War.

This new unit's name was a contraction of "American, New Caledonian Division." The name was unusual as most U.S. divisions are known by a number. After World War II, the Americal Division was officially re-designated as the 23rd Infantry Division, but it was rarely referred to by that name.

During the Vietnam conflict, the Americal Division had a bit of a bumpy record. Though it

Insignia Sleeve

Unit Insignia

performed well in numerous battles and campaigns, the American's reputation was tainted by the My Lai massacre, in which hundreds of unarmed South Vietnamese civilians were killed. The massacre was committed on March 16, 1968 by a platoon of the division's 11th Infantry Brigade, led by Second Lieutenant William Calley. It is still known as one of the most horrific incidents of violence committed against unarmed civilians during the Vietnam War.

The American was reactivated September 25, 1967 in Vietnam from a combination of units already in Vietnam and newly arrived units. Its precursor, a division-sized task force known as Task Force Oregon, was created in Quang Ngai and Quang Tin provinces from the 3rd Brigade of the 25th Infantry Division, the 1st Brigade of the 101st Airborne Division, and the 196th Light Infantry Brigade. These were all separate brigades that deployed to Vietnam in 1966.[6]

Among the American Division's many units in Vietnam were three independent light infantry brigades: The 11th Light Infantry Brigade "Jungle Warriors" from Schofield Barracks, Hawaii served primarily in the Duc Pho area; the 196th Light Infantry Brigade "Chargers" from Fort Devens, Massachusetts served primarily in the Tam Ky area; and the 198th Light Infantry Brigade "Brave and Bold" from Fort Hood, Texas served primarily in the Chu Lai area. This is where I would end up.

The American Division became the largest infantry division in the Vietnam War and its heavily contested area of operations in Quang Ngai and Quang Tin included more territory than any other division in Vietnam. It operated in diverse terrain from the mountainous central highlands, to the heavily foliaged piedmont, to the flat and open coastal plains. Its diverse missions against the Viet Cong and North Vietnamese Army included search and destroy, search and clear, rice harvest protection, and accelerated pacification.[10]

The 198th and 11th Brigades were withdrawn from Vietnam in November 1971, and the division was inactivated. The 196th Brigade was reconstituted as a separate brigade and remained in Vietnam until June 29, 1972, the last major combat unit to be withdrawn. Its 3rd Battalion, 21st Infantry (Gimlets) was the last U.S. maneuver battalion to leave Vietnam, on August 23, 1972.

For its service in Vietnam, the American Division and its units received numerous awards including the U.S. Army Presidential Unit Citation, U.S.

Navy Presidential Unit Citation, Valorous Unit Award, Meritorious Unit Award, and The Republic of Vietnam Cross of Gallantry with Palm.[10]

The shoulder sleeve insignia's four white stars on a blue field symbolize the Southern Cross under which the organization has served. The blue color stands for infantry.

On the distinctive unit insignia — also known as the unit crest — the blue saltire alludes to New Caledonia in the Southwest Pacific where the division was created and first activated on May 27, 1942. Each of the four white stars stands for the Southern Cross constellation on its division insignia, as well as the four World War II campaigns (Guadalcanal, Northern Solomons, Leyte, and Southern Philippines) in which the division participated. The anchor refers to the Navy Presidential Unit Citation awarded the division for Guadalcanal. The red arrowhead and Philippine sun stand for the assault landing, Southern Philippines, and the award of the Philippine Presidential Unit Citation. The unsheathed sword refers to Vietnam, where the division was active.

Notable Americal Division Members[6]:
H. Norman Schwarzkopf, 1969–1970
Colin Powell, 1968–1970
Tom Ridge, 1969–1970
Tracy Kidder, 1968–1969
Tim O'Brien, 1969–1970
William Calley
Ernest Medina
Marc W. Miller

ARRIVAL

After my visit to the personnel department, I was told to go out and stand in front of the dilapidated building to wait for my ride. During those fifteen minutes I began to wonder where that ride was going to take me... what my actual job description was going to be... who my boss was going to be... who the other G.I.s were there that I would be spending so much time with. As my mind drifted, I suddenly heard a loud "beep beep." And I look up to see my ride, a gray Army Jeep. In the driver's seat was Sergeant Claymon

Freeze. He seemed like a friendly enough guy and very talkative; I learned that he was from Oregon, and he began to name the folks that were working for the Americal Division's NCO/EM Open Mess system.

As we entered the actual area where the Americal Division NCO/EM Open Mess system was located, I could see the South China Sea. There were many buildings in the area, the largest being a warehouse. Sergeant Freeze drove right into the warehouse area, and I saw hundreds of pallets of beer and soda. Each pallet was made up of 1,920 cans, and these little items were worth more than gold. You see, South Vietnam is very hot and humid, and at that time refreshments were scarce. As I was to find out during my eleven-month hitch to the Americal Division, we were able to use the beer and soda as bartering items.

SFC GARDNER

SFC Addison Brown Gardner was where the buck stopped when it came to running the Americal Division's club system. When we met, he took me into his private quarters. I looked around and saw mahogany paneled walls, air-conditioning, hot and cold running water — all amenities that the normal G.I. in Chu Lai had no access to — not even close. And there I had a boss who had access to everything. It was slowly starting to sink in just how good of a position I'd landed in.

I later found out that we also had what was called the class A telephone from which we could call anywhere in Vietnam. Not even the two-star general (who at that time was Major General Charles M. Gettys) had access to this phone system. But there in the club system, we did. If Gardner wished it, he could have access to lobster and steak twice a week, or even fresh fruit such as oranges and apples, which were basically a delicacy at Chu Lai. It wasn't long before I realized that whatever my boss wanted he had the ability to get. It also wasn't long before I realized this man was a grade-A drunk. As a church boy and lifelong teetotaler, this was the first time I really found myself working closely with someone who regularly abused alcohol. It was no surprise then, that in addition to soda, we had pallet after pallet of Carling Black Label beer. Gardner, of course, usually stuck to something harder, but he knew all the G.I.s really wanted was something cold to quench their thirst and something familiar they could relate to. And what's more American than a cold beer or soda? As I said, that was worth more than gold.

Gardner began by asking lots of questions about me and my background.

He was essentially interviewing me. Unbeknownst to me at that time, there were a number of other things that he was looking at, and I would only find out in the ensuing months what these things were. Evidently, I passed the initial test, because Gardner told Freeze to take me to the hooch where my bed was.

We walked down a gravel road about twenty yards to a grouping of hooches, which were essentially small shacks. Most hooches were built for maximum occupancy, without consideration for comfort. We're talking bare bones, and I certainly didn't expect to find them equipped with amenities or creature comforts. Imagine my surprise when I walked into what were to be my living quarters and was met with a gust of refreshing, cool air. Yes, we had A/C. My hooch looked more like a little apartment back in the States than a shack in the middle of a war zone. We even had running, hot water — the only hot shower in the Americal Division. Everyone else showered in a semi-private stall under a garden hose. We really did have it good compared to the rest of the troops in Chu Lai. I even had a nice, thick mattress on my bunk; it was not as nice as what I had at home, of course, but it was without a doubt one of the most comfortable set ups in Division.

As I took in my new surroundings, Gardner told me he wanted to meet with me the next morning to introduce me to the person I was replacing, who would be leaving the day after next. That meant I was supposed to learn in twenty-four hours what this guy had done in the past eleven months.

His name was Spencer. I would later find this to be an interesting coincidence, because the first mentor I ever had after I came back from Vietnam, finished my service in the Army, and moved to Miami was also named Spencer.

Gardner told me that I was in charge and that I would report directly to him; his main concern was that I made sure the books were correct and the monthly reports were completed on time. As I began to find out more about this system, I learned that of the fifty-six clubs, thirty of them were NCO clubs, which meant that you had to be a sergeant (E5) or higher to frequent them. The thirty elite clubs had hard liquor, one of the most valuable parts of our inventory. The other twenty-six clubs, for those with a rank of specialist or corporal (E4) and below, served beer, soda, and snacks. We also had several clubs with restaurants in which the G.I.s could get a hamburger or hot dog, both coveted items in South Vietnam.

The Vietnamese club employees only got C-rations to eat, for example a chocolate bar or a can of fruit, but no fresh meat. It was the type of meal you and I would eat only if we were really hungry and out in the bush. I would come to learn that some of the Vietnamese employees were stealing food. They would take rubber bands and attach pieces of raw steak to their legs and then pass through a security point before going back into their villages. We had no clue. After a while, though, the security officials caught on and those who were stealing were permanently banned from entering the base. I found it hard to blame them, as they were basically starving people. During my first dinner at the Combat Center, before I was assigned to the American Division, I saw some Vietnamese in a dumpster, eating garbage that the G.I.s had thrown away. This was a disheartening image that remains hard to shake.

THE CLUB SYSTEM

By the end of the first day, I had met the fifteen or so folks who now worked for me, including Freeze, the one who picked me up. He'd been there the longest and would become an important figure in my life. Freeze came out of the field, where he was an 11 Bravo, and I believe endured some fairly serious wounds — a number of pieces of shrapnel in his chest and arms and head. These wounds were bad enough to take him out of the field and into the rear area, but they weren't bad enough to ship him back to the States. So, he became part of the personnel working for the club system.

If Freeze had a job description, in my mind it would have been scavenger. The club system was unique; we were not really a part of the U.S. Army organization. We had no budget. Everything we had, which included the fifty-six clubs, was all built through the bartering system. And we had to beg, borrow, and steal to build it all, which Freeze was a large part of. If Gardner wanted to build a new club, we had to "buy" the lumber, which really meant we had to barter with the Navy Seabees, who had access to just about every building material you could think of. But there was one particular commodity we had that the Seabees didn't: beer and soda. With a pallet of beer or soda, we could barter for anything we needed. SFC Jorge Perez, who ran the warehouse, had his counterpart at the Navy Seabees, which wasn't far away because their Landing Support Troop ship (LST) was on the South China Sea less than two miles from where we were located. So, the Seabees would bring their flatbed truck filled with the materials we needed, drive into our warehouse to unload, and leave with usually three pallets of a combination of beer and soda. It was considered a fair "payment."

I'll never forget one holiday in which we had a special dinner. Freeze showed up with two fully cooked turkeys, which were extremely rare to find. He had bartered with the local cook at one of the nearby units to get them. I don't know what he traded to get those two turkeys, but they were very good, and I guarantee we were the only unit within the entire U.S. Army eating turkey in South Vietnam. When it came to food, and really, most things in general, we lived better than anybody else. Comparatively, we were spoiled.

With my job description, I never pulled guard duty once I got to my unit. Even better, I never pulled KP either. During my shift, which lasted from 7:00 a.m. to 7:00 p.m., all I had to do was to ensure that we got the inventory out to the clubs. It seemed too easy, but it wouldn't be long before I encountered some unexpected challenges.

VEHICLES

Our vehicles were the backbone of our ability to service the clubs and our clientele: the soldiers of the Americal Division. When I first arrived at the club system's office compound, I noticed that the vehicles being used were painted gray and not the usual drab olive green. I asked SFC Perez, the warehouse manager, about this because he also maintained the fleet of vehicles to transport the supplies to the fifty-six clubs within the Americal Division. He informed me the gray paint on a vehicle indicated it was a salvage vehicle, which the club system was allowed to utilize.

We had seventeen military vehicles: four jeeps, six half-ton trucks, six two-ton trucks, and one wrecker truck. We also had the only civilian vehicle, a Ford 150, which stood out like a sore thumb. The Ford 150 was purchased legitimately with club funds and shipped to Chu Lai from the States. The biggest problem we had with the pickup truck was the lack of repair parts available for it, which created quite a bit of downtime while we waited for parts to arrive from the States.

Other than the Ford 150, all of our other vehicles were military issue, either retrieved from the junkyard or, in fact, stolen. Now and then, we were able to use a vehicle that was previously damaged during a firefight and repaired. However, most of our so-called "salvage" vehicles had actually been stolen by our scavenger, Freeze, on SFC Gardner's orders.

Freeze's strategy involved going to a club in the evening when soldiers were there relaxing, meeting friends, and having beers. He would survey the parking lot and determine which vehicle he was going to steal based on the vehicle type Gardner told him to look for. For example, if a two-ton truck was needed, he would find a two-ton truck.

It was actually quite simple. At that time, military vehicles did not have keys. You could simply get into a vehicle, start it up, and be on your merry way. In an effort to prevent theft, many drivers would use a heavy chain to lock down the steering wheel. The chain could only be unlocked with a key... or with our scavenger's very strong bolt cutters, which he would carry around with him to the clubs. Freeze always found a way.

Once our scavenger secured a new vehicle, he would drive it to a private area where the engine number was rubbed off and the vehicle was painted gray, becoming a part of our inventory.

While this satisfied our need for additional vehicles, it was of course a major problem for the military person originally responsible for that particular vehicle. Coming out of the club to find his vehicle gone, he would have to go back to his unit and report to his commanding officer that the vehicle he had been assigned was missing, likely after he'd spent the evening drinking, no less. This would land him in big trouble. How much trouble would depend on the commanding officer, who could opt for one or all of the following: an Article 15 (a form of non-judicial punishment), a fine, a reduction in rank (which also reduced pay), or a court-martial. If the commanding officer wanted to pursue it, a court-martial might even require the individual to repay the U.S. Army for the book value of that vehicle, and/or sentence him to thirty days in the stockade.

Now, if the fact that a division of Uncle Sam's Army stole the majority of its vehicles sounds absolutely nuts to you, remember that we were in a war zone. Everything in a war zone is temporary, possibly even your life. So, if you looked at things that way, you may have been able to see our stealing of vehicles as a victimless crime. If no one died, how wrong could it be?

Personally, my conscience never let me feel that way. When a "new" vehicle would show up, I would always think of the plight of whoever had driven that vehicle and was responsible for it prior to the theft. He was suddenly in a really bad spot, and obviously he didn't do anything wrong.

SFC RICE

The first evening that I was at the American, they held a cocktail party. I was invited to the main hooch for hors d'oeuvres and cocktails, which I would come to find out was a nightly occurrence.

It was hard to believe that we were fighting a war in a country far away from the United States with all of the amenities that were at our fingertips, simply because we were assigned to the club system. The reason for the get-together on that first evening was to say goodbye to SFC Rice, who at that time was the outgoing custodian and was being replaced by my ultimate boss, SFC Gardner. Gardner had invited me to this party so I could meet the various soldiers who were assigned to the club system. During the course of the evening, I learned an interesting bit about SFC Rice.

Evidently, he had taken a pallet of beer and proceeded to have the pallet of beer loaded into one of the club system's two-ton trucks and drove to a South Vietnamese campsite just outside the gates of the Chu Lai compound. He then sold the beer to South Vietnamese soldiers for a profit.

A pallet of beer contains 160 cases or 1,920 cans. At the time, a case of beer cost $3.60 or $0.15 per can. Rice was selling these cases of beer for $10, which meant he was pocketing $1,600. The difficulty for the South Vietnamese soldier was he had no access to the Post Exchange store (PX) and could not purchase beer or soda on his own. So even at a high cost, the South Vietnamese soldiers would buy it simply because they had no other way to get it.

It's my understanding that Rice was able to sell all of the beer to that South Vietnamese regiment very quickly. The difficulty came later, when the South Vietnamese commanding officer arrived at the outpost to find the majority of his soldiers inebriated to the point that they couldn't function. The officer raised a real stink, which led to SFC Rice being court-martialed. He was found guilty and was reduced in rank from an E7 to an E5. He was also given a hefty fine.

However, Rice had friends in high places. I was told the Commanding General of the American Division, Major General Gettys, was a close friend of his. Upon further discussion, I was told that Major General Gettys rescinded Rice's court-martial order and expunged his records. The evening that I met SFC Rice was his last in South Vietnam. He was returning to the United States and, I was told, would submit his retirement papers. Rice was probably in his late thirties or early forties at the time and had been in the service for a long time. My initial impression of Rice was he was a large, intimidating man who was used to getting his way. I was glad he would soon be gone, and that Gardner was taking his place. Gardner seemed like he would be much easier to get along with than Rice would have been, and I was looking forward to proving to Gardner that I was the right person for this job of running the day-to-day operation of the Americal Division NCO/EM Club System.

GUARD DUTY

Even from the relative comfort of the club system, I had the terrifying experience of serving overnight guard duty twice during my tenure in Vietnam. Both times I was in a pillbox, or bunker, on the edge of the South China Sea. There were usually five or six of us in that pillbox, and we would take turns being on watch. Our basic job was to see that there was no infiltration from the South China Sea into our complex. When it got dark, it was pitch black. This was a pure darkness like I'd never experienced. Without the security of being able to see what was in front of me, my mind began to play tricks. I would think I heard something or that I saw something. Soldiers were always on high alert, so even though we may have had some time off to sleep, no one really got any rest. Instead, we were desperately awaiting the first ray of sunshine to rise from east, signifying that morning had finally come. Then we could breathe a sigh of relief; guard duty was over, and we made it through another night. It was another date we could chalk off the calendar.

One of the first things I saw with the fifteen or so G.I.s who worked in the club system was that everyone had a short timer's calendar. This was a calendar that, a lot of the time, was made up of a naked lady cut into segments. The segments were colored in as each day came and went, and once a soldier has reached thirty days left in the country, they were considered a short timer. That's when some people really become paranoid. I watched many of these guys reach that elusive thirty-day mark and start doing everything they could not to go outside the compound. For the most part, they had managed to defy the odds by still being alive, but they still had to make it through thirty more days before they could board that big freedom bird home. No doubt, those final days felt twice as long.

Short Shotting

Coming from a church upbringing and a church school as strict as Bob Jones University was, I didn't drink. I didn't smoke. I didn't have any of those "nasty habits" that most G.I.s had. I was what they called a goody-two-shoes; yet, ironically, here I was responsible for an inventory of $250,000 worth of alcohol that could basically be traded for anything.

Every day the managers would bring in their money from the previous night's take in running their clubs. They were also required to bring in a few sheets that summarized their inventory and reported what they sold. Those responsible for an EM club (for E4s and below) could only serve beer, but those for an NCO club (for E5s and higher) could also serve hard liquor, meaning that also had to be accounted for in the inventory. Not being a drinker — to this day I have never consumed a can of beer in my life — I had quite a bit to learn about the clubs, liquor, and how to determine if the managers were honest or dishonest.

I had three Filipino employees, Caesar, Nestor, and Domenic, who served as our day-to-day accounting folks to check on these fifty-six managers. As I was looking over their shoulders, having been around for about a week, I saw a column that said "overage," so I asked one of the employees, Domenic Fajardo, what that meant. He explained that if the club served hard liquor, there were a couple of ways to get more than forty-three shots out of a bottle. You see, all managers were required to pay the club system for forty-three shots per bottle, but if you were crafty, you could find ways to get more shots per bottle and pocket the rest. One method was called a "short shot," which meant you put less than a full shot of liquor into the drink you were serving to the G.I. Another way was to water down the bottle of liquor, so that you got two or three more shots out of it. The trick was to be subtle enough that no one would notice if their drink wasn't quite as stiff as it should be. If a club manager took advantage of his patrons by short shotting or diluting the liquor, he could end up with about three shots per bottle that he didn't have to pay the club system for. At a dollar per drink, he could generate three more bucks a night per bottle. The club system would go through about a hundred bottles a night, meaning an additional $300 could find its way to the managers' pockets every night. The "corporate" office, me and my Filipino staff, would be none the wiser.

But the system didn't realize that there were going to be some dishonest managers, so I asked Dominic, "Okay, we've got how many clubs that serve hard liquor?" His response was twenty-six. I said, "Out of the twenty-six clubs that serve hard liquor, how many turn in the overage?" To which he responded, "Three." I asked, "What about the other twenty-three clubs?" and he just shrugged his shoulders.

It dawned on me that some of the G.I.s who ran these NCO clubs were clearly taking advantage of the system and, in essence, stealing. So shortly after this little learning experience, what this goody-two-shoes Bruce does is go out at nine o'clock one evening to the largest NCO club that generated the most money from liquor sales. I gave the manager $100 in petty cash and said, "I'll take your inventory." When I completed the inventory check I discovered an overage of more than $60 that he should have turned in. I asked him, "Why don't you turn in your overages?"

Remember that my pay grade was E4 — I was not a non-commissioned officer. While my job with the club system came with a certain amount of power, I didn't necessarily have the smarts to understand how things really worked in a war zone. I was addressing a "lifer" — a soldier who made his career in the Army — and had no business doing what I did to that club manager, a sergeant first class. I showed my lack of peripheral vision when it came to understanding what this game was all about and, even though it gave me a sense of gratification that I was doing "the right thing," I was doing something that — if I would have continued — would probably lead to an untimely end for me.

The day after my "righteous" act of attempting to save another three hundred or so bucks a day for Uncle Sam, I was approached by another sergeant first class who ran a club.

"Lauer," he said, "I need to talk to you," and we went outside. "I understand that you took inventory last night at a club where there was some overage," and I said, "That's right, I did." He said, "That's a very noble thing for you to do, but if you want to make it through your tour you may want to think twice about doing something of that nature, particularly when you — an E4 — are addressing an E7." He essentially told me that I needed to have an element of respect for those who outranked me, even though they may be doing something wrong. "If you don't give this a rest, and word gets around," he continued, "I can guarantee that you will not see the end of your tour. Do you understand me?"

That was just about all this particular NCO needed to say to knock some sense into this naïve twenty-two-year-old. The picture he painted for me left me with no doubt that my attempt to save the day was actually not such a wise move. As much as I valued doing the right thing, I valued my life more.

SLOT MACHINES

As a straight and narrow, God-fearing graduate of Bob Jones University, I didn't drink, smoke, or carouse. However, I did have one vice: I liked to gamble. It was the aspect of competition that intrigued me; betting on whatever there was to bet on. Whether it was a football game or ping pong, I simply liked the thrill of the bet. Despite my love for gambling, I was not introduced to slot machines until Vietnam. During my first week in charge of the day-to-day activities of the club system, I learned we had an inventory of 202 slot machines — the very same kind you would have seen in Las Vegas at the time.

We got the slot machines from a South Korean gentleman named Mr. Kim, who was a civilian and lived right there with us in our compound. He was the vendor responsible for keeping our 202 slot machines in operation.

It was my job as the CFO of the club system to look into the measures taken to ensure that everything was on the "up and up" in regard to usage of the slot machines in our various clubs. It was not long before this investigation yielded a couple of disturbing discoveries. There was a sheet of paper where the club manager and the nightly winners would sign off to confirm they had actually won something, and it was our job to make sure there was no collusion. Now sometimes, I'm sure, club managers would sign for their buddies even if they didn't win, but there was no real way to stop that from happening.

The real deficiency I noticed in the system was that the club managers kept the keys to the slot machines in the clubs they ran.

This was an issue because the G.I.s would buy slot tokens from the club managers and, since the managers had control of the keys, there was no internal process to keep them from stealing. The managers could take out a certain number of tokens from the machine, put them back into his inventory, and still pocket what he originally sold them for. Essentially, he would be replenishing his own stash for free.

The whole thing seemed quite fishy to me and, based on the corruption I'd experienced in Vietnam so far, I had no doubt that at least some of the managers were stealing. However, at the time, I still had no earthly idea to what degree the theft was occurring. Being the goody-two-shoes that

I was, I told my three Filipino employees to tell the managers to bring their slot machine keys to me. They would no longer have access to the machines in their clubs. I had no idea what kind of chaos this would create. Immediately, there was all kinds of muttering about me, a lowly E4 who had just been promoted to E5, who had the audacity to interfere with the operation of the clubs. It wouldn't take long to see why the managers were so up in arms — I was causing them to lose A LOT of money.

The club managers turned in paperwork on a daily basis with the revenues for the slot machines they were responsible for. Before I took the keys away, the total revenue from the 202 slot machines was between $25,000 and $30,000 a month. Of the first full month that I had control of the keys, the slot machine revenue jumped to almost $100,000 per month. That means the club managers were pocketing somewhere around $75,000 a month. Divide $75,000 by the 200 and so slot machines we had, and that's an average of about 371 bucks per month, per slot machine that was being stolen from Uncle Sam's Army.

With this little exposé of mine, I nearly created World War III. If there was ever a moment I was at risk of falling victim to "friendly fire," this was that moment. I suppose you might say I should have learned my lesson from the short shotting experience not working in my favor, but the collusion in this instance was on a much larger scale and carried much more weight in the eyes of the higher-ups.

Quite candidly, it made me feel pretty good that I had instituted controls that saved the U.S. government so much money simply by implementing some safeguards in the club operations. That $75,000 a month came out to $900,000 a year which, if you consider inflation rates, would equate to more than $3.5 million at the time this book is being written.

Although I was not a very popular person among the club managers for a while, I benefited from the quick turnover in the club system. It only took a few months before the managers I exposed were out and new ones, who were none-the-wiser, were in.

BRONZE STAR

On February 26, 1970, near the end of my tour, the U.S. Army awarded me a Bronze Star Medal for meritorious achievement in ground operations against hostile forces in the Republic of Vietnam.

The citation reads:

"By direction of the President, the Bronze Star Medal is presented to Specialist Five Frederick B. Lauer, United States Army, who distinguished himself by outstandingly meritorious service in connection with military operations against a hostile force in the Republic of Vietnam. During the period March 1969 to March 1970 he consistently manifested exemplary professionalism and initiative in obtaining outstanding results. His rapid assessment and solution of numerous problems inherent in a combat environment greatly enhanced the allied effectiveness against a determined and aggressive enemy. Despite many adversities, he invariably performed his duties in a resolute and efficient manner. Energetically applying his sound judgment and extensive knowledge, he has contributed materially to the successful accomplishment of the United States mission in the Republic of Vietnam. His loyalty, diligence and devotion to duty were in keeping with the highest traditions of the military service and reflect great credit upon himself and the United States Army."

The Bronze Star and Citation

After the U.S. Army shortened the time frame for a tour of duty in Vietnam, it became evident that, for many, the one-year stay would be shortened anywhere from fifteen to thirty days. I was scheduled to depart Vietnam on or around March 15, 1970, but I knew that time would be less. I simply didn't know by how much.

About seven months into my tour, I began meeting with Major General Lloyd B. Ramsey to brief him on the status of the club system. That meeting was held each month at his office, and I was always accompanied by the colonel of the personnel division, also known as the G1. Ramsey had a way of always putting me at ease, so I had become comfortable giving him a monthly breakdown of what transpired in the club system. He was easy to talk to and asked several pointed questions, which I always had the answer to. He seemed very interested in the controls that I had implemented in the club system during the year that I had been involved. It became evident that the general believed what I had to say and listened to my suggestions and comments regarding questions that he posed to me.

Even though I was very young, I could simply feel General Ramsey's energy and charisma. He had the unique ability to get 120 percent out of you and have you smile while doing it. He was a true "soldier's soldier" and he made me proud to be a part of the U.S. Army.

One day, the division's chief of staff sent word that I was to report to General Ramsey for what would be my fourth and final meeting with him. After I finished my briefing Ramsey asked me to stand at attention as the G1 colonel handed him a citation and pulled something out of a small box that I initially could not see. Major General Ramsey then stepped forward and said something to the effect that he enjoyed working with me for the past several months and told me that I had proven to him, without a doubt, that I was very knowledgeable of the day-to-day operations of the club system. Further, because of the involvement of the Senate subcommittee and the ongoing phone calls that he was receiving, the information that I imparted to him was very valuable in his being able to talk to various members of the subcommittee. And with that, he pinned a Bronze Star on my uniform.

I didn't really know what to say to him other than, "Thank you, sir," as it was a very humbling and proud moment for me to have received this medal and citation for my efforts to go above and beyond the call of duty. It is a moment that happened over fifty years ago, yet I remember it as if it took place yesterday.

It is evident that this soldier, Major General Lloyd B. Ramsey, was destined to be a four-star general. However, as it is addressed in his book, *A Memoir*, the general never had the opportunity to further his advancement because of the tragic helicopter crash that took place on March 17, 1970, near Chu Lai, some three weeks after I left Vietnam.[8,11]

Even though I only spent a short time during my Vietnam tour with Major General Ramsey, what he taught me was invaluable. For example, he always handled himself as a true professional, and while he was in command of 25,000-plus troops, and he was able to converse easily with the common soldier, making that individual feel important. I guess you could say that Major General Ramsey was my first mentor.

The Bronze Star is very special to me and made me cherish the eleven months and nineteen days I spent in the Republic of South Vietnam even more. My time in the Army truly laid the foundation for the thought process and overall approach to life that would serve me well in my future endeavors, both personally and professionally.

The below excerpt contains more information about the Bronze Star Medal and its significance:

"The Bronze Star Medal is the fourth-highest individual military award and the ninth-highest by order of precedence in the U.S. Military. It may be awarded for acts of heroism, acts of merit, or meritorious service in a combat zone... The Bronze Star Medal (without the "V" device) may be awarded to each member of the Armed Forces of the United States who, after 6 December 1941, was cited in orders or awarded a certificate for exemplary conduct in ground combat against an armed enemy after 7 December 1941."[7]

POKER

As strange as it may sound, Chinese salesmen would come to our base in Vietnam to sell custom-made business suits. They sold many suits per week, and the soldiers who purchased them would mail them home. I was not interested in a suit. However, I did spend some time with the salesmen.

At the time I worked from 7:00 a.m. to 7:00 p.m. for the club system. Several nights a week, after the clubs shut down, two or three of us would invite the salesmen in to play poker — for money, of course. Like I've mentioned before, gambling was my one and only vice, and in Vietnam a soldier needed a vice. Given the exceedingly poor way in which the Chinese salesmen played, part of me thinks they would lose on purpose in order to become better "friends" with us so they would be invited back and could sell more suits.

I won money gambling. While I sent my entire paycheck home to my wife, I would use some of my winnings to buy stuff. For example, I bought a camera at the PX, which was like a Best Buy for the G.I.s. I also bought a slide carousel and beautiful silk material from the Vietnamese, which I sent home. The money I won gambling was essentially my disposable income and made it possible for me to buy items that made life a little more comfortable in Vietnam, while sending home unique gifts for Barbara that she wouldn't be able to get in the States.

CPA Jon Head

While serving in Vietnam, I had two encounters with the Criminal Investigation Division, or CID, of the U.S. Army. The first encounter was eight months into my tour and was a case concerning CPA Jon Head, who worked for one of the big eight accounting firms before he was drafted, just as I did. Jon was the cashier for the club system and, therefore, responsible for the accounting of the approximately $15,000 to $18,000 per day we received from the clubs. The standard operating procedure indicated that these monies were to be deposited into the bank. We had one bank in Chu Lai, which was an American Express Bank. If you've been paying attention, it should come as no surprise that the Americal Division was the largest bank account American Express had in Chu Lai.

Well, about two months before Jon's departure, we came up missing $2,000. We never found that money and our Vietnamese cashiers were blamed. Although I don't know that they took the money, the ultimate responsibility was with the cashier, Jon, whom I believe was a very honest person, especially given his background. To this day, I don't know if the issue was ever resolved.

Nonetheless, missing $2,000 created a problem and SFC Gardner told Jon that he had two choices: replace the money, or face a court-martial. Now mind you, here's a guy who is about to leave Vietnam and terminate from the service. Suddenly being responsible for $2,000 put him in a precarious position, but he didn't have much of a choice when it came down to it. Gardner told him that he would set up a call for him — using the Military Auxiliary Radio System, or MARS — to talk to his parents first and ask if they would be willing to send the money to replenish the missing funds in the club's checking account. Gardner was one of the only people in Chu Lai who had access to a MARS phone. Jon made the call, and fortunately for him, his parents sent a check. Jon left Vietnam when he was supposed to leave, albeit $2,000 lighter, which I'm sure left a bitter taste in his mouth. To my knowledge, Jon was a great soldier and did everything he was supposed to do. This was just an unfortunate incident.

PROSTITUTION

Prostitution within the Americal Division compound played a small part in the ongoing debauchery and corruption that affected the club system. The first bits of information I received regarding prostitution within our club system came from a warrant officer. A warrant officer is a technical expert in a specific career field and ranks above an enlisted person and below a commissioned officer. This warrant officer, for the most part, flew helicopters and had flown me in junkets to various landing zones where we would set up an operation for the day for the G.I.s to get something cold to drink. Landing zones were remote from the main camps and were very dangerous. They were surrounded by barbed wire to keep the Vietnamese out and had trip flares that would go off when intruders penetrated the fence. We were able to land the helicopter within the confines of the landing zone. More than once we were fogged in and forced to spend the night inside the landing zone at a place called L.Z. Baldy. We were scared senseless as we heard flares get triggered.

Once, at a barbecue, this warrant officer showed me a number of pictures of naked women. Most of the women were South Vietnamese and were in compromising positions. It was immediately clear these pictures were taken within one of our clubs. The warrant officer warned me that there were three civilians currently in Chu Lai who were sent by the Senate subcommittee to investigate corruption within the club system. I would cross paths with these three civilians a few days later when they visited our office. Somehow the Senate subcommittee folks got hold of some of these pictures, which added to the ongoing investigation of the club system.

My understanding from the warrant officer was that certain clubs — I believe there were only three of them that were actively participating in this illegal activity — would secretly stay open beyond the usual nine o'clock closing. A line would form around the club, which had essentially become a brothel, to service the G.I.s. Quite candidly, a G.I. did not know if he was going to be alive twenty-four hours from now and most of these men were 11 Bravos. Money did not mean much to them, but a few minutes of "intimacy" with a woman did, considering it could be their last chance.

It is my understanding that once the commanding officers were notified of this extracurricular activity, those who were actively participating in promoting it were hunted down and taken care of accordingly. I believe that this illegal activity was only operational for a few weeks, but in that time those involved managed to make a lot of money, with each encounter costing fifty dollars. The entrepreneurship of the G.I. looking to make a buck in Vietnam always amazed me. While it may not always have been ethical, it was very creative and far-reaching.

A Visit From Two 16s and One 17

As I mentioned, my warrant officer friend had told me to expect visitors of a civilian nature. Sure enough, within the next few days, three gentlemen dressed in suits with white shirts and ties paid a visit to our hooch. Now, I was in the back part of our office and I could see these three gentlemen stood out like sore thumbs because of their attire. No one wears a suit and a tie in a war zone, but here these three were, and they looked very serious. I heard them ask one of my Filipino workers who was in charge and he turned around and pointed at me. The three gentlemen came forward and introduced themselves and pulled out shiny, very official looking gold and blue badges that indicated their rank within the government system. Two were GS-16s and one was a GS-17. To understand what that means, here's some background on what the Army's pay scale looked like.

The General Schedule (GS) is the predominant pay scale within the United States civil service. Currently, the GS is separated into fifteen grades, GS-1, GS-2, etc. up to GS-15. However, at time, there were also three GS "supergrades" — GS-16, GS-17, and GS-18. These grades were eliminated under the provisions of the Civil Service Reform Act of 1978, but in 1968, they were given only to very important people. With nearly the highest possible pay grades, those three gentlemen were the equivalent of two major generals and a lieutenant general.

Of course, standing there looking at these badges, I had no idea what I was dealing with, but it was quite evident that these gentlemen were on a mission and that my boss, SFC Gardner, was about to become very uncomfortable. The senior guy asked me who my boss was and where they might find him. I told them I would find SFC Gardner, but that it might take me a few minutes and that they should stay right where they were. They agreed and I hustled back to the hooch where SFC Gardner resided.

Now mind you, it was only about 10:00 a.m. and my boss rarely surfaced to the outside world before noon. As I journeyed back to find him, my heart was racing, and I knew that this was no ordinary situation. I knocked on Gardner's door, and I heard his groggy response saying, "Yeah?" I let him know in a very loud voice that there were two GS-16s and a GS-17 in our front office looking for him. Gardner's response was immediate and very clear. He said he would be there in five minutes.

I went back to our front office and told these three gentlemen that SFC Gardner would be with them shortly and asked them to take a seat. It was obvious that they didn't want me around listening to whatever they had to say, so I left them alone. It took Gardner closer to ten minutes than five, but when he showed up, I was astounded by his crisp, pressed khaki uniform adorned with all of his ribbons and highly shined shoes. I mean, he actually looked like a professional soldier for once. The only item out of place was the pair of sunglasses he had on. The obvious reason for the sunglasses was his very, very bloodshot eyes, having earned them the night before with all of his drinking. I heard the lead guy ask Gardner, "Is there a place we can go and not be interrupted?" Gardner then took these three gentlemen back to his hooch, which had his own private, paneled-wall office, which obviously looked out of character in a war zone.

Gardner never offered any information regarding the gist of their conversation, but he was noticeably nervous and fidgety. Over the next few weeks, he became much more secluded and very rarely did we see him come out of his hooch. It was as if he was biding his time.

BOARD OF DIRECTORS

The Board of Directors of the club system met once a month. My boss, SFC Gardner, would hold the Board of Directors meeting in various club locations. The Board was made up of five command sergeants major, thirty-year veterans nicknamed "white sidewalls," a name given to senior members of the military for their short-sided haircuts that had often gone grey or white. These were true professionals who knew what they were doing and were an integral part — if not the backbone — of the Army. Another term for them could be "spit and polish."

I would come to find out that the reason the Board of Directors existed was to keep SFC Gardner's backside out of hot water. The Board would vote on approving certain large purchases Gardner made throughout the year. I was the secretary for the Board of Directors, and it was my job to take notes, follow up on things, and communicate with the sergeants major on an ongoing basis. Part of my job in setting up each monthly meeting was to make sure I understood what each command sergeant major's favorite liquor was. Accordingly, I would bring a case of their preferred liquor, like Seagram's Gin, Crown Royal, or Johnny Walker Black. Whatever they wanted we could get. Instead of money, they were paid with a whole case of liquor for their time each month that they met with us.

When a command sergeant major would rotate off of the Board of Directors because he was going back stateside, he was replaced. I will never forget the first meeting that Command Sergeant Major Miller attended. He came to our meeting and about midway through, he stood up and said to SFC Gardner, "I want nothing to do with this. This is a waste of my time. I don't like the way this smells. You'll not see me again. You can find somebody else." Then he said he needed a ride back to his unit. SFC Gardner looked at me and said, "Please take the command sergeant major back to his unit." Which I did.

During the time that I was with CSM Miller, he looked at me and said, "Son, you need to be very careful because what your boss is doing is at the very least suspicious and doesn't smell right. You need to be very careful about what you do and how you do it." I'll never forget those words. He turned out to be right.

Soon, the heat really started coming down as the Senate subcommittee began investigating the club system. The two GS-16s and GS-17 who had earlier paid Gardner a visit had focused their attention on the various large purchases made by the club system. They found out that all of these purchases had been authorized by the Board of Directors, whether it was the purchase of $50,000 worth of Polish sausage or $50,000 worth of Christmas cards, everything had been approved. In addition, we made several purchases of nice furniture and fixtures, all of which were approved by the Board of Directors.

Little did we all know at the time that the suspiciously large purchases were part of a grander scheme led by the Sergeant Major of the Military Assistance Command at the time, William O. Wooldridge. It would soon come out that Wooldridge, along with several co-conspirators, had set up a company called Maradem to sell supplies to the club system and turn quite a profit for himself and cronies. Wooldridge had men in on his scheme who ran the various club systems throughout the world. As you may have guessed, Gardner was one of them.

Through Maradem, Wooldridge would charge the clubs many times what the items should have cost, then kick back some of the money to his custodian friends who made the over-priced purchases as a reward, while pocketing the rest. The whole thing allegedly started when Wooldridge was serving as Sergeant Major of the Army, aka the top enlisted position in the Army. He held that position until September 1968 — coincidentally, the same month I was drafted — and then returned to Vietnam as Sergeant Major of the Military Assistance Command. He eventually testified that he used his influence to strengthen Maradem's position and that he was fully aware that the company was paying kickbacks to club custodians around 5 percent to 10 percent of purchase price. For someone as high ranking as Wooldridge to be involved in this level of corruption was a major, national scandal.

As part of the investigation, Gardner was held for ten days in Chu Lai for questioning. I never saw him again after that, and I do not know much about what went on between him and the men leading the investigation, but it's my understanding that he got off without being charged with anything. With the help of the Board of Directors, it seemed Gardner sufficiently covered all of his tracks and made sure his activities were protected.

By this time, Gardner's tour was coming to end and it's my guess that instead of re-upping, he walked and returned to civilian life. This decision would have appeared very odd to anyone without knowledge of Gardner's alleged involvement in the Maradem scandal, considering he was nearing twenty years of service. If he'd stayed another year and a half or so, he would have received much better military benefits and been set for life. The fact that he walked away from that, in my opinion, indicates that he either was coerced to leave, or knew he'd have a higher chance of being caught if he stuck around.

Of course, I had no idea about the scale of this collusion at the time or how much of it was really going on while I was serving as secretary for the Board of Directors. Although I was not an actual decision-making member of the Board of Directors and had no power in approving expenses, the later realization of what had been going on left a nasty taste in my mouth. It was incredibly disheartening to learn that these thirty-year veterans, who were supposed to be the most loyal and patriotic of them all, had played a part in this major scandal.

ENTERTAINMENT

As mentioned before, we had fifty-six clubs located throughout the Chu Lai complex, some of them very large and some of them very small. In addition to alcoholic beverages, the clubs provided a source of entertainment for the G.I.s. We had live performers at various clubs every night. The entertainment groups provided good things and bad things. The good thing was it took the G.I.s' minds out of the war and gave them an hour or so of entertainment — singing, dancing, etc. Most of the performers were Filipino or South Korean and could barely speak English, but they could make music and that was all that mattered. Every now and then, we would have Australian or even American performers. These groups, which were referred to as "round eyes," typically drew a bigger crowd than the Asian performers. But no matter the race or nationality of the performers, the entertainment took some of the harshness of war off the G.I.s' minds for at least a short period of time.

However, hosting the entertainment also came with challenges, through no fault of the performers themselves. Let's just say that some of the G.I.s were a little too tempted by the female entertainers. It was so extreme that we had to build a separate complex with a twelve-foot-high barrier fence and post guards in front of it to keep the entertainment groups out of harm's way. Even with those precautions in place, there were still some instances in which an enlisted guy would have too much to drink and attempt to truly go above and beyond in pursuing his interest with a female entertainer. Quite a few men attempted to climb that twelve-foot-fence, though I am not sure if any succeeded.

Another dilemma associated with the entertainment, which was unknown to me at the time, occurred when Gardner was still in charge. Apparently, he'd been making special deals with the booking agents. As you can imagine, Gardner had tremendous power because he could pick and choose who he wanted to work with. If the booking agents didn't cooperate, then their clients didn't work in the Americal club system.

This all came to light after Gardner left and was replaced by SFC Thomas Leatherwood, who became my new boss. Leatherwood was a true infantryman and therefore had no experience with the club system. One day, he came to me and said, "Lauer, I've got three months left. Keep my ass out of trouble and I'll sign anything you need signed, but I don't want any problems." My response was, "SFC Leatherwood, I have got your backside covered."

In one of his first days on the job, Leatherwood came to me and his face was white as snow. He said, "Lauer, I had a booking agent come to see me, and he wanted to know if I wanted the same 'deal' as Gardner had." I looked at Leatherwood and said, "I don't know what kind of deal you're talking about." And that was the truth. Leatherwood went on to explain that the booking agent told him they were paid a whopping $350 per show. There were three entertainment groups that each did two shows a night, so if I do the multiplication correctly, we were spending $2,100 a night, or approximately $65,000 a month, for entertainment. The booking agent went on to tell Leatherwood that Gardner was also charging the agents as part of this deal. Each of the agents was paying Gardner $50 per show they were booked for. That means Gardner was making a $300 kickback every night, or about $9,000 a month, with this scheme of his.

It should also be noted that before his sudden departure, Gardner had been taking a trip to Hong Kong every month. At the time, I hadn't thought much of those trips, and found it easier to stay out of it. However, as Leatherwood explained this situation with the booking agents, Gardner's mysterious monthly trips suddenly made more sense. With his rank, Gardner had the ability to do just about anything he wanted. Getting orders cut that allowed him to go to Hong Kong once a month wouldn't have been very difficult. My guess, based upon putting two and two together, is that each month he was taking his dirty money and depositing it outside of Vietnam.

Overall, from my point of view, the entertainment groups were a very positive influence for the soldiers. The entertainers were over there to help take the edge off the stress the G.I.s were under from being out in the boonies. Unfortunately, like many other things in life, the entertainment from a monetary standpoint was exploited, and Gardner took full advantage of it.

R&R

During my time in South Vietnam, there was a special week that my wife and I were looking forward to spending together. I was able to take some leave, and we met during the week of Thanksgiving in Oahu, Hawaii. We spent seven days at the beautiful Ilikai Hotel on the famous Waikiki Beach. The difficult thing was knowing that I had four months remaining in my Vietnam tour, and would soon have to say goodbye to my wife and dodge bullets again for the near future. Getting back on the plane headed to Chu Lai, I was nauseated and full of dread that I might never get to get back to the States and back to my wife, who was and is still the love of my life.

When I set foot back on Vietnamese soil, my senses were all of a sudden on edge again, and the thought of survival was constantly on my mind. I became more obsessed than ever with a strong urge to remain alive. From this point on, I was always on high alert. The closer I got to the end of my tour, back to my beloved USA, the more my whole being was focused on survival.

BOB HOPE

One of the biggest events during my tour in Chu Lai was Bob Hope's performance at Christmastime. In our case, it was Christmas Eve 1969 that Hope came to Chu Lai and put on his program for the soldiers. The anticipation and the actual performance by Hope and the entertainers he brought with him was priceless for every G.I. in need of a few minutes to enjoy themselves and not think about the war. Security was tight and most of the time the soldiers had maybe an hour or so advance notice that Hope was going to be there. You can imagine the security concerns about thousands of G.I.s congregating in a concentrated area and wanting to get a glimpse of the great Bob Hope. But in Chu Lai, it was pulled off without a hitch and it was one of the most memorable events from my time in Vietnam. Seeing Bob Hope perform on center stage is one of a few good memories that many veterans took home from Chu Lai and share today.

MY FRIEND MCWEENIE

The other encounter with the Criminal Investigation Division was much more serious than the incident with poor Jon Head. It started with a phone call I received from the American Express Bank in Hong Kong. The caller wanted to validate two checks that were being presented for payment, for a total of about $42,000. The amount was not unusual. However, the individual in command of these two checks wanted to cash them immediately, which rightfully made the teller suspicious. The teller got his boss, and his boss called me to ask what I knew about this particular situation.

I asked my cashier to give me the checkbook that would "house" the two checks, both of which were in the 600 series. Instantly I knew we had a problem because we were only into the 200s in our current checkbook. You see, our checkbooks had one hundred checks to a book, with four checks to a page. They were kept in a safe that only the cashier had access to. At that time, the cashier was a guy named Bob Sprauge, who had a master's degree and was a very competent individual. I asked Sprague to open the safe and bring the 600 series of checks to me and quickly saw that four checks were missing. This was extremely abnormal and meant that someone had actually chosen four random checks from the book and removed them. I immediately told the banker who I was speaking with to detain the person trying to cash the checks. However, apparently the amount of time that had lapsed while we were checking into the situation made that individual nervous. He left the two checks as he ran out of the bank and we never apprehended him.

Leatherwood had come and gone, and my boss at this time was a gentleman by the name of SFC Guy Walker. When I explained the situation to Walker, he said there was only one option: to bring in the Criminal Investigative Division of the U.S. Army to solve the problem. Now I'm about nine months into my tour and I'm beginning to get short timer-itis. I'm really concerned that if I get caught up in this investigation, I won't leave Chu Lai on time. There was a possibility they could have kept me there for as long as the investigation took.

I will never forget the morning after my boss made the call to the CID. A Jeep rolled up to our office and out stepped a very tall man, who was hugely obese, and had on an Army uniform with a name tag that read "McWeenie." I swear I am not embellishing here for comedic effect. His lapel showed no rank, so we didn't know if he was a private, a corporal, or an officer. One of the potential problems for me was there were only three of us who knew who the signatories were for the checks, and I was one of those three.

I was shown a facsimile of the checks that the mystery man had attempted to cash in Hong Kong and the signatures matched beautifully with the signature cards. The only reason the bank called from Hong Kong was because of how nervous of the person trying to cash the checks seemed, and the fact that he wanted the actual cash.

Well, McWeenie rounds up me and my entire staff, including the warehouse personnel, and we all start signing checks. We signed standing up and sitting down, both right-handed and left-handed. This was McWeenie's attempt to gather evidence for his expert who would perform an analysis of our signatures to see if one matched as the culprit.

McWeenie became my "best friend," as he was down almost every day for the next forty-five days. Meanwhile, the days were ticking off until it was time for me to leave Chu Lai, and McWeenie's constant presence certainly did not make the time go faster. Fortunately, my fear of having my stay extended while the case was ongoing did not come true. Although the case was still unresolved on my scheduled departure date, it fortunately did not hold things up for me as I'd feared it might. I am unsure of the outcome, but personally, I believe that it was an inside job. What I mean by that is the folks in Saigon with American Express Bank shipped these ten books with one-hundred checks to a book, and we never looked through each book to see if all the checks were there. We simply took the checkbooks and put them in a safe under the supervision of the cashier. In retrospect, it makes sense that someone at the bank in Saigon, where these checks originated, could have neatly removed four checks from the 600 series and, because he had access to the signature cards, was able to forge signatures on the checks to be able to cash them. The other two checks missing from that 600 series were never found, and, to the best of my knowledge, no one ever attempted to cash them. That was probably out of fear of what happened with the first two checks. This ordeal turned out to be yet another instance of corruption that was not solved, although the one difference is that one of our own may not have been at fault this time.

Exit

When you become a short timer, with less than thirty days in your tour, each day feels longer than the last. You've worked so hard to avoid the many potholes and pitfalls of being in Vietnam thus far, but one mistake or attack could wreck it all. You're on high alert and don't want to do anything to put yourself in the path of harm. You stick close to your hooch, and you might not even go to the PX. You don't want to expose yourself to anything that could jeopardize your departure, and you become paranoid hearing all sorts of rumors about things that could do just that. In my case, I got orders that allowed me to leave eleven days early. This might not sound like a lot, but as the days grew longer the closer I got to my exit, eleven days felt like a lifetime. That time meant a lot.

I packed my duffel and got a ride to the airport to board a C1-30 plane headed for Cam Ranh Bay, a city best known for its beaches and tourism, where the chances of an attack were very slim compared to Chu Lai. I was told it would take two days for me to be processed, and I would then fly home on a civilian plane. While I was boarding, my mind went right back to the moment I first landed in Vietnam and heard the tremendous roar of the soldiers who were about to embark on their journey home. At that time, it was hard to picture myself as part of this group, celebrating the end of their tour in Vietnam. But there I was. It was my turn to board the "big freedom bird." I had made it, but it was hard not to think about those who hadn't.

We landed in Fort Lewis, Washington, and went through a debriefing process. They took our measurements to get us new khaki uniforms with our "lettuce," meaning all the new badges and medals we acquired in Vietnam. It was a fairly benign process. There was no fanfare or no welcome party. At that time, no one was thanking veterans and active members of the military for their service. In fact, off base, you almost felt despised. I remember the tension present when I went to the airport in Seattle to get a ticket to Cleveland, Ohio. My uniform drew attention, which included sneers from those who disagreed with the Vietnam conflict. I had even heard of soldiers being spit on. But mostly, in my case, it was just a lack of acknowledgment. At best, it was a very discomforting feeling — the lack of appreciation from the very people you risked your life to keep safe.

It was a relief when I finally saw Barbara along with her brother Jerry and his wife Rosalie, who were at the airport to greet me with the first smiling faces I'd seen all day. Barbara did not know about my early return until after I landed in Seattle. Being able to call her and tell her I was home, and safe, was a moment I will never forget.

CHAPTER 7

FORT BENNING, GEORGIA

Upon returning stateside, I still had eighteen months left to serve, but all those returning from Vietnam were given thirty days of leave. I spent most of this time at my mother's house in Ohio, where Barbara had been living. Toward the end of my leave, we packed our belongings into a U-Haul, which we hooked to the back of the '68 Pontiac Lemans that I had bought just before I was drafted. Soon, we were off to Fort Benning, Georgia, to start the next chapter of our lives. As a benefit of my rank as a sergeant, we were offered housing on base. We lived in a six-unit townhouse building. Although I had it about as easy as one could in Chu Lai, returning to the States, where I had a real roof over my head, was an adjustment. It was hard to shake the feeling of being constantly on the alert. Any loud sound had me diving for the ground to avoid an imaginary gunshot or a stray piece of shrapnel. It had become an innate reflex and it probably took a year for me to completely break the habit.

One of our first nights in Fort Benning, my eleven months and nineteen days in Chu Lai shone through in a less than flattering way. Barbara said something superfluous that I must have not agreed with. I can't remember what it was, but my response to her was "At ease." She quickly put me back in my place, saying, "I am not one of your soldier boys. You don't talk to me like that." And that was the last time I said anything like that to her.

Payroll MOS at Fort Benning

When I arrived at Fort Benning and went to sign in, my records indicated that I had a finance MOS. The NCO signing me in, Master Sergeant Dinkle, was an E8 — and as the paygrades only go as high as E9, he was pretty high up. It was apparent to him that I had no finance training, and therefore, he asked how I could have this MOS. In truth, a friend of mine had changed my MOS for me. This friend was one of the part-time club system managers who worked in personnel. One day he came in to drop off some money and said, "I looked you up and you have a supply MOS. Do you want me to change it?" I asked, "You can do that?" He assured me he could, so I said sure. When he asked me what to change it to, I said finance, even though I didn't have the military credentials. Despite the hassle I was now facing, this would prove to be a very helpful MOS.

While the E8 was giving me a hard time, clearly skeptical of my ability to do the job, a "full bird" colonel walked in, Colonel Van Der Lyke. It was lucky for me that he did. The E8 showed him my records and described the situation, probably thinking the colonel would agree with him and have my MOS changed back to supply. However, upon seeing that I was employed by Price Waterhouse, the colonel responded that I could train to do this job in three weeks, and that the E8 should move forward with my placement.

Had this not happened and had I stayed with my supply MOS, I most likely would have been assigned to the 196th Light Infantry Brigade as a supply sergeant — which would have been very different from the cushy lifestyle my finance MOS afforded me. Over the next thirteen months, I had a pretty good set up. I pulled guard duty maybe twice, but there was no real risk of a break-in at the finance office, although I did have to carry an M14 rifle. For the rest of my time in the Army, I did not have to partake in any other undesirable — or dangerous — tasks.

Next Door Neighbor – Payroll

One Saturday at my home on the base, I got a knock on my door. It was my next-door neighbor, who was a big, burly, African American man. When I answered, he told me that he had not gotten paid that week. I was in charge of payroll at the time and knew that everyone in the system got paid — and he was in the system. He then revealed the truth: that he had lost all of his paycheck playing craps.

His biggest concern was that his wife would find out. Truthfully, I did not have much sympathy for him, but as someone who enjoys gambling, I could see how he could get himself into such a predicament. I said I would not tell his wife, so long as she did not come over and ask. I then suggested that on Monday he request an advance for 50 percent of his next paycheck, which I believe he did. This was the only time my neighbor came to my door with such a request.

COURT MARTIAL OF A CAPTAIN

Every eight weeks there would be a new class of recruits in OCS (Officer Training School). Get-togethers were held to welcome the new recruits along with their wives. At some point, it came to light that the captain in charge of OCS was propositioning the officer candidates' wives during these gatherings. He would be alone with one of the women and would say something to the effect of, "Your husband is not doing that great, but if you 'work' with me, it may improve his chances." The captain's inappropriate behavior was discovered after a few of the women compared stories. He was subsequently court martialed and, as a punishment, he lost his position. However, he was simply reprimanded, then transferred. Had he been a civilian, I suspect his punishment would have been much more severe.

MAJOR STAMP

If someone has been in the service for a long time, it is expected that they will rise in the ranks. If they do not, one might aptly describe them as "a dud." When I met Major Stamp, he had been in the service for twenty-four years, but had not advanced past the rank of major. He was a "lifer" and it appeared he didn't have much to do other than harass me. Major Stamp reported to my boss, Colonel Latham, the Officer in Charge (OIC) of the 196th Light Infantry Brigade, so he would come in and check on the records. Despite being a "dud," his shoes were always spit-polished.

Major Stamp had a beef with me because here I was, this finance guy with a bronze star, who had been in the Army for a mere fraction of the time he had. I assume it was his jealousy that drove him to constantly irritate me, always nit-picking and treating me poorly. There was clearly a reason this guy had not made it past the rank of major.

Near the end of my term, Major Stamp had really gotten under my skin, and I decided to get back at him. I removed him from the payroll system in mid-September, timing it with my departure on September 20, so that by the time the next pay period rolled around, on September 30, I would be gone. I also gave Major Stamp's payroll records to a buddy of mine, who sent them to Korea. I can only imagine that when Major Stamp did not get paid, and my replacement could not locate his records, that it was quite a scene.

COURT MARTIAL OF A PFC

At Fort Benning, there was a mechanic who worked on helicopters. One day, he decided to try flying one of them, which he was not authorized to do. When he was only a few feet off the ground, he panicked and crashed the helicopter. At the time he was a private first class (E3) — but not for long.

He was immediately demoted to private (E1), and I had to cut his wages by two thirds and apply that to the amount of the cost of fixing the helicopter.

At that time, an E1 earned about $67 per month, which for him, was reduced. The cost to fix the helicopter was $167,000. At that rate of repayment of approximately $42 per month, without any interest being applied, it would have taken him 331 years to repay the debt. If he had kept his nose clean in the stockade, his case might have been reviewed, the debt expunged, and he would have been given a dishonorable discharge. However, I do not know the final outcome of the situation.

FATHERHOOD

At the time, it was my wife Barbara's intention to be a businesswoman. She came to Fort Benning and began to look for work in nearby Columbus, Georgia. However, she was unable to do so because she was sick.

When I took my wife to the Army doctor, complaining of nausea, he told us that she wasn't deathly ill as we had feared. In fact, there was nothing wrong with her at all. She was pregnant. This came as an unexpected yet welcomed surprise.

Barbara continued to feel sick for the first three months of her pregnancy. All you had to do was say the word "meat" and she would throw up. On her delivery date, once contractions started, I drove her to Martin Army Hospital. The hospital staff told me to go home and they would call me, which was customary in those days. I dropped her off at 6:00 a.m. on January 3 and got the call to return at 2:30 p.m. When I arrived, the nurse asked me if I'd like to see my child, who was in the nursery. I followed, but when she pointed to a pink bassinet, I knew there must be some mistake. Up until that moment, I was convinced we were having a boy. It was a sobering moment, and I was filled with pride. We had a little girl, Heather, and she became the apple of my eye.

Following the birth of our first child, my wife's mother came down to live with us and help out. This was in January of 1971. I am very thankful that my wife spent that time with her mother, for only one year later, in February of 1972, Barbara's mother passed from a malignant brain tumor, which struck only sixty days prior to her demise.

Making matters worse, her father had died of a heart attack just eight months earlier. Both were only forty-eight years old. After the death of Barbara's mother, we became the guardian of my wife's twelve-year-old sister, Mary Ann. This time of our lives was forever changed, as we were now responsible, at the ages of twenty-five and twenty-six, for a twelve-year-old, in addition to our eighteen-month-old, Heather. This was something that we had never anticipated, but nevertheless we were going to have to adjust our lives accordingly.

Quite candidly, I believe that my time in the Army helped both my wife and I cope with this newfound responsibility, and better equipped us to deal with the emotions of a twelve-year-old who had just lost both of her parents.

CHAPTER 8

RETURN TO CIVILIAN LIFE

I officially left the Army in September of 1971. When my service was complete, I returned to Ohio and to my position at Price Waterhouse. Barbara and I, with our young daughter, found an apartment in Galloway, a suburb of Columbus. Compared to some of my fellow soldiers who had served on battlefields, my adjustment back to civilian life was fairly smooth. It helped that the last eighteen months of my service were spent on U.S. soil in Fort Benning, Georgia. I was also privileged to have had a sound career to return to at Price Waterhouse, a sure thing to depend on. For many of my fellow veterans, it was not so easy.

PRICE WATERHOUSE

When Price Waterhouse found out that I had been drafted in September of 1968, my tenure with them ended until my days in the U.S. Army were over. The company held my job, and I returned to work there approximately three years later.

In 1971, I was assigned to the Borden's account, a huge dairy company that is still around today. It was the first year that Price Waterhouse was auditing this particular company.

Despite my love of accounting, I quickly discovered that I did not like public accounting. Auditors are nobody's favorite person, and I did not like the stigma of being someone who would get employees in trouble for accounting errors. To add to that, the managing partner I worked under grilled me about my time in the service and why I didn't pursue the path of officer candidate school. Frankly, I did not think that was of any concern to him, and it rubbed me the wrong way.

The combination of these factors led me to the realization that working for Price Waterhouse was not, in fact, my "dream job." This was somewhat ironic, considering that for most of my time at Fort Benning, I painstakingly counted down the days until I could return to my job there and truly begin my career as a civilian.

Although it did not turn out as expected, I am grateful for the experience I had at Price Waterhouse, as it allowed me to provide for my family and secure the means to find my true passion. Fortunately, I knew the accounting profession was universal and would not be hard to find a new career path, especially with the magic words "Price Waterhouse" on my résumé.

In addition to not being so keen on public accounting, I also decided I did not like the cold, and neither did Barbara. So, in March of 1972, we moved to Florida. One month earlier, my wife's mother had passed — the second parent she'd lost in just eight months. For Barbara and me, moving to Florida served as a much-needed fresh start.

ALLEN MORRIS COMPANY

My high school buddy Tom Getz, who I mentioned was a conscientious objector in Vietnam earlier in this story, is the reason I ended up in commercial real estate. After returning from Vietnam, Tom went on to earn his master's degree in real estate from the University of Florida. He worked on Brickell Avenue in Miami, a prime spot in a prime city when it came to commercial real estate.

In 1972, Tom introduced me to the Allen Morris Company, known to this day as the "grandfather" of Miami real estate. Just several years earlier, in 1968, Allen Morris had broken ground on the first multi-tenant office building in Brickell, an area near downtown Miami that up until that point, was considered "no man's land."

Today, Brickell Avenue is known as the "Wall Street of Latin America" due to its accessibility to Central and South America and its significant international presence. It is now home to numerous international, national, and regional headquarters for major companies, including Bank of America International, which resides in that first building developed by Allen Morris, known as the 1000 Brickell Building.

Needless to say, Allen Morris was the company to be with when it came to commercial real estate in Miami at this time. Tom helped me get an accounting job there, and I did the books for a number of Allen Morris' closely held corporations, mostly high-rise office buildings. I knew nothing of commercial real estate at the time, but it wasn't long before I started to gain an understanding of the industry. And I fell in love with it.

I remember being completely enamored with Mr. Morris and his ability to make money. And boy, did he make money. Since I was in charge of the books, I was able to see all of the company's purchases. At one point, I noticed he bought a new Porsche, but I never saw the vehicle in person. Turns out, it belonged to his son, Allen Morris Jr., who was born with a silver spoon in his mouth. Eventually, after four years of working long, hard sixty- to seventy-hour weeks, it started to wear on me. The nature of my job allowed me to see exactly how much money I was personally making for the Allen Morris Company, and how little of it was making it into my pocket. The differential did not sit well with me, and I decided I would prefer a job where I would have more control over my income.

Nonetheless, I am extremely grateful for my experience with Allen Morris. My direct boss was a gentleman named Bill Spencer, who became my first mentor in the commercial real estate industry. Although I only worked for him for four years, we kept our friendship intact, and forty years later, after maintaining this long-standing relationship, I attended his funeral in Roswell, Georgia. This gentleman gave me the opportunity to come to Florida and begin a new career that I loved, and for that I am forever thankful. He also taught me discipline, integrity, and work ethic.

CLARK-BIONDI AND EARL STARR

I learned a lot working at Allen Morris, but one of the most significant takeaways from my time there was the realization that I wanted to start my own firm. In February of 1976, I became one for the four founding partners of Clark-Biondi, a Miami-based real estate firm specializing in commercial sales and leasing.

At its height, Clark-Biondi had grown to employ 150 people with more than 3.2 million square feet of commercial property under management in Miami, Boca Raton, Tampa, and Sarasota. We kept the company for a little over ten years, until Grubb & Ellis, a national firm based in California, acquired us.

Clark-Biondi was a company that, in many regards, should not have succeeded. We had no capital and little experience running a company. But what we did have was determination and the ability to work hard.

Although my family never missed a meal, things were tight during that first year. Hotdogs and peanut butter sandwiches became staples in our household. Barbara, who had been staying home with our children, started babysitting out of our home to provide supplemental income.

A man named Earl Starr was an important figure in turning things around for us. Earl worked at Prudential in Miami. I cold called him for eighteen months. Finally, he gave me the opportunity to bid on a project against two other management firms that were both well-established and much larger than us. We put many hours into preparing our presentation and brought our A-game to the meeting. Our hard work and extra effort paid off, and we won the assignment from Prudential. From that moment on, we never looked back, as we continually proved that Earl Starr made the right decision hiring our firm.

That first assignment was in the fall of 1978, and I still have the Prudential account today, forty-one years later. This is a career accomplishment that I am very proud of and thankful for.

After twenty-eight years at Prudential, Earl left to become part of the John Alden Life Insurance Company (JALIC). He called me the very next day and said he needed my help re-negotiating their corporate lease. My response was, "Who are you working for?" There were a number of four-letter words before he gave me his answer.

"John Alden," he said. "Do you know who John Alden is?" I replied, "I don't have a clue." He said, "Before you come down to Miami tomorrow (I was four hours away in Tampa at the time), you'll know who John Alden is."

At Earl's insistence, I looked John Alden up in the encyclopedia. I learned that he came across on the Mayflower and was the second in command of the colonies. He had nine children and died in 1667. Clearly, Earl did not actually work for John Alden himself, but for a company founded in this man's name. It seemed important to him, so I made sure to study up on my history before the meeting.

I asked Earl to provide more details to prepare for the meeting. He said the company currently was in a ten-story building with 15,000 square feet per floor. They occupied the entire building, a total of 150,000 square feet. In this well-located area of Miami, it was quite a big deal.

The next day, I was in Mr. Starr's office. He was very disgruntled because he had just received a phone call the day before from the landlord indicating that the John Alden Company had missed the notification period to renew their existing lease. This made the deal somewhat complicated. The landlord's representative was out of New York, a gentleman by the name of Benedict, whose last name I only know was phonetically pronounced Tak-a-shoe-ski. Benedict was holding the company's feet to the fire by not allowing them to renew, which brought into consideration the possibility of moving. Now, to move a 150,000-square-foot tenant within a twelve-month period is extremely difficult because you have to find another, open location to move to, design and build out the space, and negotiate the lease within the tenant's means. Fortunately, there were twelve buildings to choose from in Miami's Central Business District. One of these buildings was owned by Prudential, a company Earl and I of course knew very well. After talking to several potential landlords and looking internally within JALIC, it became apparent that our existing requirement for a 150,000-square-foot lease ultimately became a 180,000-square-foot lease in another, better building.

After his initial phone call with Benedict, I was instructed by Mr. Starr not to have any conversations with him. Once we had the lease under review for the new location, Mr. Starr told me to call Benedict and let him know that we wanted to meet with him. Benedict agreed. At this meeting, Mr. Starr informed Benedict that JALIC would be vacating the entire building at the end of the expiration period. At this time, JALIC was within seven months of the lease end. We had our own construction company at Clark-Biondi and knew we could build out the space. There was a very awkward silence that seemed to last forever. Finally, Benedict said something to the effect of, "Mr. Starr, is there not any way we can salvage this situation?" Mr. Starr looked at Benedict directly and said, "You had your chance, you treated us like scum, and we are moving out." And we did. I heard later that Benedict was terminated. My guess is that he took a building that was worth, conservatively, $22 million and reduced it to nearly nothing by losing its sole tenant.

Earl Starr allowed me the opportunity to represent JALIC in all of their lease renewals and to negotiate all of their new leases throughout the United States. The largest deal I had the privilege of doing for John Alden was a 251,000-square-foot, twenty-year lease in Miami. Quite candidly, I should have a portrait of Earl Starr hanging in every room of my house, for he literally put me on the commercial real estate map. As I told Rod Santomassimo in his book *Brokers Who Dominate*, Earl taught me the importance of providing the highest quality of service and of making your client look good — especially to his boss. He also urged the importance of making every client feel like they're your only client. "If you make them look good, they'll keep coming back and they're going to tell their friends," he told me. "That's another way you build up businesses, through service and integrity and doing what you said you were going to do when you're supposed to do it.... When you do that, you build relationships and loyalty... The payoff is repeat business and referrals and being able to bypass the 'beauty contest' competition with other brokers."

JAMES VINCENT SANTOMASSIMO

It was during my time with Clark-Biondi that I developed a relationship with another gentleman who would have a significant impact on my career, James Vincent Santomassimo. James hailed from Long Island, New York and served as an asset manager for the owner of one the main office buildings that Clark-Biondi was leasing and managing. I remember James taking copious, detailed notes during meetings, which he could recall or refer to as needed. This was an important lesson to me. James was all about fairness and professionalism. He also emphasized top-quality service, holding himself and everyone else to the standard that, within reason, "the day is not over until your client is happy and satisfied." James was a mentor to me, and I am honored to have later served as a mentor to his son, Rod, who worked as a broker for my company CLW, in the early 1990s. I am honored to be one of the "industry veterans" profiled in Rod's book, *Brokers Who Dominate: 8 Traits of Top Producers*, published in 2011.

CLW

After selling Clark-Biondi to Grubb & Ellis, three of the four original owners of Clark-Biondi, myself included, waited out the three-year noncompete with Grubb & Ellis, and in 1988, formed a new full-service real estate company called CLW.

Once we got CLW off the ground, one of my partners, Will Wilkins, became insistent that we needed new blood. I disagreed. However, thanks to Will's persistence, we eventually welcomed Lou Varsames and Doug Rothschild, both of whom had been making a name for themselves early in their real estate careers. The four of us made up the primary leadership of CLW for the majority of the company's existence. CLW grew to become a national, full-service commercial real estate firm providing office, industrial, senior housing, property, and corporate services throughout the United States. In 2013, CLW was sold to Cassidy Turley, which then became DTZ, and was eventually acquired by Cushman & Wakefield in 2015.

RECOGNITION AND SUCCESS

I mentioned earlier in this book that I returned from Vietnam at a time when there was a stigma associated with the war. The Vietnam conflict had a reputation issue and veterans were not typically appreciated the way they are today. A soldier in uniform was more often met with indifference, if not a sneer, than a salute or a "thank you." I'd grown accustomed to this attitude, until about three years ago when my son gifted me a hat with "Vietnam Vet" embroidered across the top. I instantly received a "thank you for your service" the first time I wore it. This caught me completely off guard, as it was so rare to be thanked by a stranger. I continue to wear this hat regularly, and someone comes up to say thank me for my service nearly every time. Of course, I wear this hat because I am proud, not because I am seeking gratitude, but it does feel good to be recognized and appreciated after so many years of being overlooked.

Recognition and reputation have been important themes in my professional career as well. Over the years, I have had time to ponder the meaning of success. One thing I've learned in my nearly five decades in this business is that success means different things for different people. A lot of people measure success based on what their bank account looks like. This might work for some people, but I think for most people, or at least for me, monetary success alone is not truly fulfilling. For me, it has always been more important to be recognized for my abilities and integrity than for the number of zeros on a commission check. In this business, your reputation is everything, and it's the one thing that you will inevitably leave behind. One of the best measures of my own success has come in the form of recognition from my peers for the reputation I have built. I feel this every time a friend in the industry picks up the phone to ask me to work with them, or to simply ask me for my insight and advice. In 2018, I received the pinnacle of this type of recognition when I was inducted into the Hall of Fame of the National Association of Office and Industrial Parks' (NAIOP) Tampa Chapter. The professionals who received that honor before me include people I consider icons in the industry, and who I trust and respect. For me, there is no greater form of career success than being recognized among those I respect.

CAREER REFLECTIONS

As I finish this book, it has now been nearly fifty years since my time in the Army came to an end. I often think about how military service prepared me for the rest of my life. I had led such a protected and sheltered life in my youth and young adulthood that, had I not been quickly exposed to the "real world" through my time in the Army, I don't know that I would have fared as well. While I will never forget the camaraderie and friendships, it was the many instances of graft, greed, and corruption I experienced that were the most formative. The Army not only hardened me, it made me smarter. My service gave me both the thick skin and sharp wit I needed to make it in an industry that can be cut-throat at times.

CLOSING THOUGHTS

One of the most important things the Army taught me was how to use peripheral vision. I mean that both literally, as in being able to spot a stray piece of shrapnel barreling toward me from the side, as well as figuratively, in that it taught me to look at the bigger picture. I learned to consider the implications of my actions, or someone else's, not just in the moment, but well into the future. In the Army, this helped me stay out of harm's way. In civilian life, and in my career in commercial real estate, it helped become a strategic decision maker and critical thinker. When I deal with my clients today, I have to think about what I want to accomplish, how I am going to accomplish it, who I am going to go to, and how my dealings with one client or contact may affect my other business relationships and future pursuits.

In commercial real estate, and many professions, you have to think five steps ahead to anticipate your clients' needs and make the best decisions for all parties involved, all while keeping an edge on the competition.

The Army also taught me how to address the chain of command. It showed me that loyalty, honesty, and integrity could go a long way in building valuable, mutually beneficial relationships. In a business development role, you have to know how to get in the door, but what's even more important, and often more difficult, is knowing how to stay there once you're in. Relationships are key in this business. To develop strong relationships, you have to know how to make a great first impression, and then deliver on the promises with an exceptional level of service.

Although I spent just three years and one week in the Army, it was undoubtedly one of the most formative and important experiences of my life. There are times when I feel as though it was just yesterday that I, as a naive, recent college graduate who was raised in the church, found myself boarding that Boeing 737 jet to Vietnam with absolutely no clue what I was about to get into. There are other times when I am simply astonished by how much the world has changed and how much I have been able to experience over the last five decades. Not a day goes by, however, that I am not utterly grateful for the beautiful family that was given to me, and for all those who fought so hard for our freedom.

APPENDIX

STATISTICS FROM THE VIETNAM WALL

- There are 58,267 names now listed on that polished black wall, including those added in 2010.
- The names are arranged in the order in which they were taken from us by date, and within each date the names are alphabetized.
- The first known casualty was Richard B. Fitzgibbon, of North Weymouth, Massachusetts, listed by the U.S. Department of Defense as having been killed on June 8, 1956. His name is on the Wall with that of his son, Marine Corps Lance Cpl. Richard B. Fitzgibbon III, who was killed on September 7, 1965.
- There are three sets of fathers and sons on the Wall.
- Of those listed on the Wall, 39,996 were just 22 or younger, and 8,283 were just nineteen years old.
- The largest age group, 33,103, were eighteen years old.
- Twelve soldiers on the Wall were seventeen years old.
- Five soldiers on the Wall were sixteen years old.
- One soldier, PFC Dan Bullock, was fifteen years old.
- On their first day in Vietnam, 997 soldiers were killed.

- On what was scheduled to be their last day in Vietnam, 1,448 soldiers were killed.
- Thirty-one sets of brothers are on the Wall.
- Thirty-one sets of parents lost two of their sons.
- Fifty-sour soldiers attended Thomas Edison High School in Philadelphia.
- Eight women are on the Wall, and they died nursing the wounded.
- During the Vietnam War, 244 soldiers were awarded the Medal of Honor; 153 of them are on the Wall.
- Beallsville, Ohio, with a population of 475, lost 6 of her sons.
- West Virginia had the highest casualty rate per capita in the nation. There are 711 West Virginians on the Wall.
- The Marines of Morenci — They led some of the scrappiest high school football and basketball teams that the little Arizona copper town of Morenci (population 5,058) had ever known and cheered. They enjoyed roaring beer busts. In quieter moments, they rode horses along the Coronado Trail and stalked deer in the Apache National Forest. And in the patriotic camaraderie typical of Morenci's mining families, the nine graduates of Morenci High enlisted as a group in the Marine Corps. Their service began on Independence Day, 1966. Only three returned home.
- The Buddies of Midvale — LeRoy Tafoya, Jimmy Martinez, and Tom Gonzales were all boyhood friends and lived on three consecutive streets in Midvale, Utah: Fifth, Sixth and Seventh Avenues. They lived only a few yards apart. They played ball at the adjacent sandlot ball field. And they all went to Vietnam. In a span of sixteen dark days in late 1967, all three would be killed. LeRoy was killed on Wednesday, November 22, the fourth anniversary of John F. Kennedy's assassination. Jimmy died less than twenty-four hours later on Thanksgiving Day. Tom was shot dead assaulting the enemy on December 7, Pearl Harbor Remembrance Day.
- The most casualty deaths for a single day was on January 31, 1968 — 245 deaths.
- The most casualty deaths for a single month was May of 1968 — 2,415 casualties were incurred.
- For most Americans who read this they will only see the numbers

that the Vietnam War created. To those of us who survived the war, and to the families of those who did not, we see the faces, and we feel the pain that these numbers created. We are, until we too pass away, haunted with these numbers, because they were our friends, fathers, husbands, wives, sons, and daughters. There are no noble wars, just noble warriors.

GLOSSARY

Term	Definition
AFB	Air Force Base
AWOL	Absent Without Leave
CID	Criminal Investigative Division
CO	Commanding Officer
CSM	Command Sergeant Major
G.I.	A member of the U.S. Army. The initials have stood for Government Issue, General Infantry, and originally Galvanized Iron
GS	General Schedule
KP	Kitchen Police
LST	Landing Support Troop
Shipped	Kicked out of school
OCS	Officer Candidate School
OIC	Officer in Charge
MOS	Military Occupational Specialty (job description)
MP	Military Police
NCO/EM	Non-Commissioned Officer / Enlisted Man
PFC	Private First Class
PX	Post Exchange, a store on a military base
QM	Quartermaster School
RSVN	Republic of South Vietnam
SFC	Sergeant First Class

ACKNOWLEDGEMENTS / CITATIONS

Articles, Websites:

1. http://vietnam-casualties.findthedata.org/d/b/Ohio/Mansfield
2. http://www.virtualwall.org/dd/DenigJH01a.htm
3. http://www.virtualwall.org/dd/DenigJH01b.htm
4. http://www.VirtualWall.org/dw/WinderDF01a.htm
5. American Division. http://en.wikipedia.org/wiki/23rd_Infantry_Division_(United_States)
6. http://en.wikipedia.org/wiki/American-Division
7. http://en.wikipedia.org/wiki/Bronze_Star_Medal
8. http://www.a-1-6.org "Rescue of a Downed General," Wayne R. Johnston, 1st Bn 6th Inf 1970-71.
9. http://en.wikipedia.org/wiki/General_Schedule_(US_civil_service_pay_scale)
10. https://americalfoundation.org/cmsalf/

Books:

Ramsey, Lloyd B. *A Memoir*. Clinton County Historical Society. 2006.
Murphy, Edward F. *Vietnam Medal of Honor Heroes*. Presidio Press. 2005
Santomassimo, Rod. *Brokers Who Dominate*. Domus Publishing. 2011.

Photographs:

- Photo #1 — Carved Boat Sculpture, taken by F. Bruce Lauer November 1969 in Vietnam
- Photos #2A through #2E — *The Talon*, the 1964 Malabar Senior High School Yearbook, Volume I, from Mansfield, Ohio
  - Photo #2A — Joseph Denig
  - Photo #2B — David Winder
  - Photo #2C — David Beard
  - Photo #2D — F. Bruce Lauer
  - Photo #2E — Thomas Getz
- Photos #3, #4 — American Insignias. http://en.wikipedia.org/wiki/23rd_Infantry_Division_(United_States)
- Photo #5 — Framed Bronze Star and Certificate, Photo by Kimberly Satterfield and Kristin Bodin

ABOUT THE AUTHOR

F. Bruce Lauer is a father of four and grandfather of nine. He currently lives in Florida with his wife of 50 years, Barbara. Bruce earned a B.S. in Accounting from Bob Jones University and a B.S. in Finance from the University of Miami. He served in the U.S. Army from 1968 to 1971 and was awarded the Bronze Star in 1970 for his service in the American Division in the Republic of South Vietnam.

Bruce began his career in accounting with Price Waterhouse in 1968, then entered the commercial real estate industry where he became co-owner of Clark-Biondi Company in 1976. Bruce grew the firm's property management to seven million square feet of office, industrial and retail space in South Florida before selling the company to Grubb & Ellis in 1985. In 1988 he co-founded CLW Real Estate Services Group and held the role of Principal until he sold that company in 2005. Bruce currently serves as Vice Chairman of Cushman & Wakefield.

A leader in his community, he has served as a Board Member and Secretary of Morton Plant Mease Hospital Foundation, a member of the CEO Council of Tampa Bay, a Board of Directors Member for the Outback Bowl, a Board Advisor to the Family Enterprise Center of Stetson University, and an adjunct professor for the Graduate Program at Florida International University in Miami, Florida.

Bruce also holds several professional affiliations, including Certified Property Manager (CPM), Licensed Real Estate Broker in the state of Florida, and former Certified Public Accountant (CPA).

This is Bruce's first book. He is also featured in Rod Santomassimo's book, *Brokers Who Dominate*.

ABOUT THE PUBLISHER, TACTICAL 16

Tactical 16 Publishing is an unconventional publisher that understands the therapeutic value inherent in writing. We help veterans, first responders, and their families and friends to tell their stories using their words.

We are on a mission to capture the history of America's heroes: stories about sacrifices during chaos, humor amid tragedy, and victories learned from experiences not readily recreated—real stories from real people.

Tactical16 has published books in leadership, business, fiction, and children's genres. We produce all types of works, from self-help to memoirs that preserve unique stories not yet told.

You don't have to be a polished author to join our ranks. If you can write with passion and be unapologetic, we want to talk. Go to Tactical16.com to contact us and to learn more.

CPSIA information can be obtained
at www.ICGtesting.com
Printed in the USA
BVHW021437070920
588053BV00001B/3